The
Collectors' Book
of English Antiques

The
Collectors' Book
of English Antiques

Geoffrey Wills
and
Edward T. Joy

South Brunswick and New York:
A. S. Barnes and Company

Originally published in two volumes. *The Book of English Furniture* © 1964 by Edward T. Joy. *The Book of English China* © 1964 by Cyril Staal.

A. S. Barnes and Co., Inc.
Cranbury, New Jersey 08512

ISBN 0-498-01431-2
Printed in the U.S.A.

The Collectors' Book of English Antiques is actually two books in one. The first section deals with furniture and is followed by a second section on china. Each section is complete in itself and is numbered separately from the other section.

THE
BOOK OF
ENGLISH FURNITURE

Contents

List of Plates

LINE DRAWINGS IN TEXT

ACKNOWLEDGMENTS

The author wishes to express his gratitude to the following for their generous help with the illustrations (a large number of which are appearing for the first time) and for much valuable advice:

Norman Adams Ltd; Plates 27, 31, 35, 50, 51, 52, 54, 55, 62, 69, 70, 71, 72, 73, 74, 77, 82, 90, 93, 94, 96, 97, 98.

Michael Barnes, Esq.: Figures 1, 2, 3, 4, 5, 6, 7, 8, 9.

Edward Barnsley, Esq.: Plates 132, 133, 134, 135.

H. Blairman & Sons Ltd: Plates 95, 99, 100.

Country Life Ltd.: Frontispiece, Plate 103.

Messrs Heal's of Tottenham Court Road, London: Plates 120, 121, 122, 123, 124, 125.

Hotspur Ltd: Plates 17, 18, 24, 32, 33, 39, 40, 41, 42, 43, 44, 46, 53, 56, 57, 58, 59, 60, 64, 65, 66, 67, 75, 76, 79, 80, 84, 85, 86, 87, 88, 89.

Mrs Wallace Hughes: Plate 106.

H. W. Keil Ltd: Plates 10, 19, 20, 21, 23, 25, 26, 29.

Alan Peters, Esq.: Plate 136

Phillips of Hitchin, Ltd: Plates 28, 30, 34, 36, 45, 48, 49, 61, 63, 68, 78, 81, 83.

Gordon Russell Ltd: Plates 126, 127, 128, 129, 130, 131.

S. W. Wolsey Ltd: Plates 1, 2, 3, 4, 5, 6, 7, 8, 9, 11, 12, 13, 14, 15, 16, 22.

Temple Williams Ltd: Plates 91, 92

J. Barbee Winston, Esq., New Orleans, U.S.A.: Plates 37, 38, 47 (from his collection of early mahogany furniture).

Victoria and Albert Museum: Plates 108, 109, 110, 111, 113, 114, 115, 116, 117, 118, 119.

Bruce Whineray, Esq.: Plates 101, 102, 104, 105, 107, 112.

Introduction

This book traces the development of English furniture from 1500 to the present day. The problems facing the designers and makers of furniture (often, but not necessarily, the same men), and their success or failure in solving them, must always be related to the social conditions of the craftsmen's times, and to the materials and techniques at their command. Both these points have been considered in this survey, and brief explanations have been made of developments in construction and decoration.

It will be noticed that although English craftsmen have always been quick to absorb foreign influences (just as foreign craftsmen have borrowed from us), their traditional approach has been to use the most suitable materials and methods in a direct way. For this reason, to stop this survey short at 1830, the accepted limit for antique furniture, would be to miss many interesting subsequent developments, such as the revival of craftsmanship in the period of the Arts and Crafts Movement (when English furniture was admired throughout Europe), and the struggle to achieve good design in the greatly changed conditions of the 20th century.

In fact, a study of antique furniture is given even more value if the appreciation of design and skill which it encourages can be applied dispassionately to the consideration of modern furniture, whose designers, after all, face very much the same problems as did their predecessors.

For the interest and information of readers, I have included, as Appendices, a glossary of technical and decorative terms pertaining to furniture, and glossaries of woods used in furniture-making (a) prior to 1830 and (b) from 1830 onwards.

Oak Furniture: *c.*1500-1660

The 'age of oak' is the traditional name for the period from early medieval times to *c.* 1660 when this timber was the principal material for furniture. The wood was converted by first felling and quartering the trunk (i.e., splitting it along its length into four sections), then cutting each quarter towards the centre, along the lines of the medullary rays, which produce the characteristic silver grain or figure of oak, and make it more durable and less inclined to warp (Fig. 1). Until the later

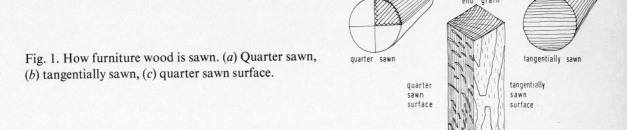

Fig. 1. How furniture wood is sawn. (*a*) Quarter sawn, (*b*) tangentially sawn, (*c*) quarter sawn surface.

Tudor period it was usual to split the log with beetle and wedge, and to trim the riven wood with the adze; the later method was to have the wood sawn across the top of a saw-pit by two men, the top and bottom sawyer, operating a large two-handed saw above and below the log.

In spite of great care taken over seasoning, oak was still liable to move in the atmosphere. In early oak pieces such as boarded chests (which were composed of six boards), the planks were fastened together by nails or oak pins, a method which persisted in country areas until the 18th century. But pinning allowed no freedom of movement in the wood, which often split across the grain. To remedy this, the panel and frame construction was used for chests, chairs and doored furniture. Oak panels were tapered on all sides to fit into deep, narrow grooves in a rectangular framework composed of horizontal rails and vertical stiles. These were united by the mortise and tenon joint, a projecting

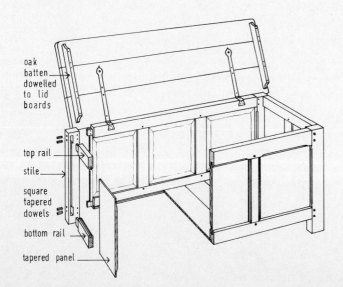

Fig. 2. Panelled chest construction.

1. Oak boarded chest decorated with 'chip' carving; there are traces of polychrome decoration. Late 15th century.

section (the tenon) of the rail being fitted into a corresponding socket (the mortise) of the stile, and secured by squared and tapered oak pegs driven through round holes (Fig. 2). The panel now had sufficient room to move and so was much less liable to warp.

This method, introduced into England from Flanders in the 15th century, amounted to a technical revolution. 'Joined' furniture now made by the joiner was lighter, stronger and better proportioned than that made previously by the carpenter.

Early Tudor, 1485–1558. Early Tudor furniture retained many of the characteristics of the furniture made in the Middle Ages, when it was designed to be carted about from place to place as its owners—king, barons, churchmen—moved about the country. It was largely the exclusive possession of the rich, who at first were slow to absorb the new ideas of the Renaissance and to adapt themselves to the increased opportunities for domestic comfort. Thus movable pieces like chests, folding chairs, stools, benches and trestle tables were prominent in large houses where social life still centred in the

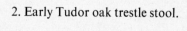

2. Early Tudor oak trestle stool.

3. Early 16th-century oak bench.

4. Early Tudor oak chair; back carved with medallioned head in profile.

5. Oak trestle dining table. Early 16th century.

great hall. Much of the best furniture, however, was imported, or made in England by foreign joiners.

The chest was the most important medieval piece, for it could be used as a seat, bed or table as well as for storage and transport. Boarded chests, of the early type of six boards nailed or pinned together (Plate 1), were still being made with, however, thinner boards, about three quarters of an inch thick. Another type of chest, of the kind made since the 13th century, had the front and back made of three planks, the central one being framed and pegged into grooves in the other two, which were lengthened to form feet. The panelled chest (Plate 12) was only gradually adopted, and was comparatively rare until Queen Elizabeth I's reign. Other varieties of chest were the hutch, a box-like receptacle with doors on legs, the standard, a large travelling chest and the coffer, of smaller size. The best coffers were made by cofferers, who covered them with leather and other valuable materials, and also made and covered other pieces of furniture.

Throughout the Tudor period stools, forms (or benches) (Plates 2, 3) and settles (i.e., forms with arms and backs) were the usual seats; 'stool', in fact, was the normal term for a seat for one person. Chairs (Plate 4), comparatively rare pieces, were symbols of authority and reserved for the heads of households or for distinguished guests. Joined chairs had panelled backs, seats and arms; 'X chairs' were often covered with rich materials and found only in great houses; turned (or 'thrown') chairs were made by turners and had triangular seats and legs, arms, backs and supports formed of turned members. 'Thrown' work by turners was distinct from 'joined' work, as turners did not use the mortise and tenon joint, but fitted the ends of turned sections into sockets.

A newer kind of lighter panelled chair, the caquetoire (or caqueteuse), had a narrow panelled back and was open under the seat and arms; it was intended for parlours and bedrooms and was based on French originals.

Trestle tables—boards (or tops) on trestle supports—of medieval type continued to be made (Plate 5). Some trestles were kept in position by one or two stretchers (i.e., cross-rails) which passed through the trestles and were fastened outside them by oak wedges. These wedges could easily be removed and the trestles stored away. The table tops or boards were massive planks secured by

6. Elizabethan draw table with bulb supports of 'cup and cover' form; frieze decorated with guilloches.

battens on the under side. But an indication of more settled social conditions was the growing use of the joined table (or table dormant), with its top fixed permanently to the underframing, and its legs connected by stretchers just above ground level.

More convenient still was the draw table, which made its appearance about 1550. A small plank was fixed across the centre of the underframe of the table, and on each side were the two smaller draw-leaves which lay, when the table was closed, under the main table top. Each draw-leaf pulled out on two runners fixed in slots in the table frame; these runners were so sloped that the extended draw-leaf came to rest level with the main table top, and they also had small blocks on them which rested against the table frame to prevent the leaves coming out too far. This draw-leaf principle, by which the table top can be extended to almost double its length, is still used today in table construction (Plate 6).

'Cupboards' mentioned in early Tudor inventories were not the doored structures as now understood, for in its original meaning a 'cup-board' was a table or shelf for displaying the family plate to visitors. But it seems clear that sections at least of some of these open shelves were enclosed, for there are references to 'close cupboards' and 'cupboards with aumbries'. An aumbry was an old term for any space enclosed by a door or for a doored compartment in a larger piece of furniture; it also came to mean a doored receptacle in which the almoner of a great house kept broken meats to distribute to the poor. By 1500 such houses also had food cupboards, with doors pierced for ventilation, and livery cupboards for storing the food and drink delivered daily to retainers, though there is no certain evidence that these latter cupboards had doors.

There were, in addition, hall and parlour cupboards in two stages, sometimes only the upper stage, sometimes both stages, being enclosed (the completely enclosed type is now referred to as a 'press cupboard', Plate 11); and presses, tall doored pieces containing shelves for clothes and linen. But it is important to note that 'cupboard' did not have its modern sense until the end of the Tudor period (Plate 7).

The bed was the most valuable piece of furniture on account of its costly hangings and bedding,

7. Open tiered oak 'cup-board' with canted sides.

8. Early Tudor bed with elaborately carved head board and foot posts; illustrated by Henry Shaw in *Specimens of Ancient Furniture* (1836).

9. Elizabethan walnut armchair, decorated with inlay.

which covered the plain wooden framework. Until the early 16th century the hangings were suspended from a canopy of rich material which was attached to the ceiling by cords. Then four corner posts came into use, with a panelled head board (Plate 8). It seems that the suspended canopy was retained until it was replaced, about 1550, by a wooden tester resting on the posts.

There is evidence that from medieval times until 1550 furniture was painted both to preserve the wood and to brighten the interior. Carved ornament was rich but somewhat coarsely executed, and often showed an incongruous mixture of traditional and Renaissance motives, the latter having been introduced under Henry VIII by Italian craftsmen. Panels were carved with Gothic tracery and 'linenfold' patterns, as well as with profile medallioned heads, vases, scrolls and other attempts at classical decoration. Much ornament took the form of shallow 'chip' carving with chisel and gouge (Plate 1).

Late Tudor or Elizabethan, 1558–1603. The vigour of national life in Elizabeth I's reign was reflected in the ostentatious decoration of its furniture, just as its growing wealth was reflected in the greater variety of furniture now found in the large houses being built or renovated with more comfortable interiors. In new houses, which no longer had defence as the prime consideration, the great hall was replaced by the great chamber, long gallery and more private rooms for the family.

After the Reformation the tenuous links with Italy were severed, and the Renaissance reached England in its florid Flemish and German versions, made widely familiar through imported pattern books of printed designs. The most characteristic decorative features were strapwork (i.e., arabesques and geometrical interlacing), arcading, chequer and floral inlay, and elaborate 'bulbs' (Plates 6, 10). Inlay was done by cutting the required pattern from the ground to a depth of about an eighth of an inch and fitting in pieces of wood of similar pattern and contrasting colours. For this purpose coloured woods were employed, including holly, bog oak, sycamore, poplar, beech, ash, yew and fruit woods. The 'bulbs', which had obvious resemblances to the puffed sleeves and trunks of Elizabethan costume, were built up by gluing sections to a central post on cupboard supports, bedposts, legs of dining tables, etc. They often had an Ionic capital at the top and were divided by a moulding into a 'cup and cover' form (Plate 6).

B

10. Oak splay-fronted cupboard with lion and bulb supports, decorated with inlay, split balusters, gadrooning and lunettes. Early 17th century.

11. Press cupboard with lozenge decoration on the panels, and lunettes on the frieze.

12. Oak panelled chest, decorated with carved arcading, guilloches (on the stiles) and lozenge ornament (on the sides) Early 17th century.

The growing use of glass windows led to the abandonment of the old custom of painting furniture, which was now inlaid with varied coloured woods, or upholstered (in the case of seats), or waxed and varnished. The search for colour led to the use of imported tapestries and carpets for wall coverings, and of rich materials for upholstery. Joiners were now using more woods, including walnut, chestnut, birch and cedar.

Joined chairs with panelled backs were made in greater numbers towards the end of the century. They became lighter and more open, losing the panel beneath the seat and arms (Plate 9). The front legs were turned in baluster shapes (i.e., like columns) and continued upwards to support the arms; back legs remained rectangular in section. Many chairs were inlaid with coloured woods. By 1600 the top rail, instead of being tenoned between the uprights, began to extend above them, with brackets ('ears') added at the sides. Richly upholstered seating furniture was also becoming more plentiful, the upholstery in some cases covering the softwood framework.

After 1550 joined stools with four turned legs began to replace the type with solid splayed ends; these legs, which were joined to deep rails beneath the seat, and to stretcher rails just above floor level, straddled outwards. Stools and benches were often made in sets to go with a table.

For about a century after 1550 two types of cupboard were generally used for service at meals in large households. One, the court cupboard, preserved the old meaning of a stand for plate and dishes, for it consisted of three open tiers or shelves, the top two being supported at the front corners by bulbous columns. Sometimes the space above the middle shelf had a doored compartment (Plate 10). The other type (the press cupboard) (Plate 11) was larger than the court cupboard, and had two stages, the lower one having shelves enclosed by doors, the upper a shallow recessed cupboard which was sometimes splayed at the sides to give more shelf space.

Draw tables (Plate 6), long dining tables with fixed tops and six or eight legs, and side tables with four or six legs, were all richly carved. So were the great beds, heavy and ornate structures, with the tester now supported, not on four posts, but on the panelled head board and on two bulbous foot posts which stood independent of the low bed frame.

Many chests were inlaid with grotesques, animals and representations of buildings. A special kind, known as 'Nonsuch chests', were inlaid with coloured woods in the shape of a palace, said, without authority, to resemble Henry VIII's palace of Nonsuch in Surrey.

13. Small oak table with drawer; bobbin-turned legs
and stretchers; carved lunette decoration on frieze.
First half of 17th century.

14. Armchair, *c*.1625, with original 'Turkey work'
upholstery.

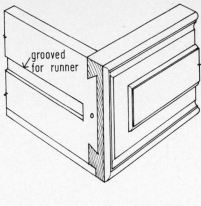

Fig. 3. Drawer construction. First half 17th century. Crude dovetail.

15. Chair, Yorkshire-Derbyshire type; c.1650.

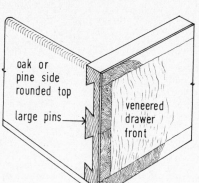

Fig. 4. Drawer construction. Second half 17th century. Also shows veneered drawer front.

Early Stuart, 1603–60. The first half of the 17th century marks the climax of the 'age of oak'. Under the patronage of James I (1603–25) and the cultured Charles I (1625–49) the architect Inigo Jones introduced true Italian architecture in the Palladian style to England, but progress in architecture, interior decoration and furniture was slowed down by Charles's quarrel with parliament. There were, nevertheless, interesting developments in chairs, chests of drawers and tables.

In James I's reign, from which the term 'Jacobean' derives, there was a tendency to tone down some of the excessive ornament of Elizabethan furniture, and 'bulbs' became more slender. There was still, however, much strapwork in low relief, floral decoration, and carving of lunettes, arcading, guilloches, etc. (Plates 12, 13). Simpler decoration became apparent under Charles I, and particularly in the Commonwealth period (1649–60), when Puritan austerity was the rule.

A decorative feature of the time was the split baluster. The member was turned to the required shape, then split down the middle; the matching pairs were usually stained black and glued to the surface of the piece (Plates 10, 15). Chests, which were still important, especially in country areas, had panelled backs and sides, and larger ones had panelled lids also. Arched panels were a characteristic of the period (Plate 12). Panel corners were mitred—i.e., each edge of the mouldings framing the panel was cut at an angle of 45°, these mouldings being run on separate pieces of oak and glued into position.

In the early years of the 17th century the best chairs of 'X frame' type had elaborate upholstery richly trimmed. Joined chairs often had arched and inlaid panels. Distinct innovations were 'back stools', the first chairs to be made without arms, among which were the so-called 'farthingale chairs', said to have been made for women wearing the fashionable farthingales (hooped skirts) of James's reign.

About 1650 appeared the type known as Yorkshire-Derbyshire chairs, which had their backs filled with two flat hooped rails, or with an arcading of balusters (Plate 15). The austerity of Cromwell's regime was reflected in the introduction of plain chairs with seats and back panels covered with leather or some other simple material, secured to the frame by brass-headed studs.

16. Table with folding top and bobbin turned legs; *c*.1650.

The chest of drawers in its earliest form appeared before 1650. Drawers, then known as 'tills' or 'drawing boxes', had been fitted to cabinets and travelling coffers from *c*.1550, and before 1600 the 'mule chest', with a single drawer at the bottom, came into use, making it much easier to reach lower layers of linen, clothing, etc. Later, two or more drawers, sometimes enclosed by doors, were placed below the box-like upper section with its hinged lid, but this hybrid type was not common until *c*. 1650 (Plate 25).

At about the same time the first true chest of drawers appeared in the form of a narrow drawer at the top, a single deep drawer beneath this, and three long drawers behind panelled doors at the base. A little later the lower doors were omitted, thus making a complete chest of drawers, but still with the deep upper drawer.

These pieces were often decorated with applied mouldings and split balusters, and inlaid with bone and mother-of-pearl. The stout oak drawer sides, which were nailed to the fronts, had grooves made in them so that they could slide along runners (or bearers) fixed to the inside framing. By 1650 the sides were joined to the front of the drawer by crude dovetails. In time the number of such dovetails increased, and they became more slender (Figs. 3, 4).

Gate-leg tables were found in many early Stuart households, developed from the oak tables with folding tops and pivoted supports which had been known since the 15th century (Plate 16). In these earlier tables one of the legs was halved vertically and framed to stretchers of half thickness so that it could swing out to support the unfolded top. In the later tables each gate was composed of two legs connected at the top and bottom by stretchers, one leg being pivoted to the table frame. The gates were swung out to support the flaps which were fastened to the fixed centre of the table by wrought iron hinges (these were nailed on until screws came into use after 1650). By means of halvings (i.e., matching sockets in the stretchers of the main framing and in the bottom of the swing-out leg) the legs could shut tight when not in use.

The Walnut Period: *c.* 1660-1750

After 1660 numbers of foreign craftsmen, particularly from the Low Countries and France (including Huguenots fleeing from religious persecution after the revocation of the Edict of Nantes in 1685) came to work in England, some of them at the court, and they passed on to English craftsmen their latest constructional techniques and decorative processes. By 1700 there was considerably more specialisation among English furniture-makers, who were now sub-divided into cabinet-makers, chair-makers, clock-case-makers, upholsterers, japanners, gilders, carvers, etc.

Veneers, Marquetry and Parquetry. From *c.*1660 to *c.*1750 the fashionable furniture wood was walnut, which is particularly associated with the technique of veneering, the process by which thin sheets of sawn wood—the veneers—were glued to the flush surface of the 'carcase', or solid frame, so that the figure of the wood could show to advantage. This new method required such careful preparation and execution that a new class of specialist craftsmen—the cabinet-makers—came into existence.

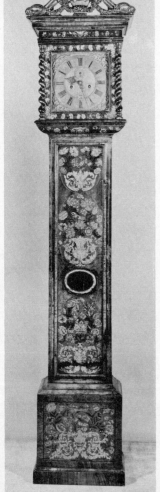

17. Long-case clock decorated with floral marquetry in various woods; *c.*1685.

18. Side table with twist-turned legs and curved flat stretchers, decorated with marquetry; *c.*1685.

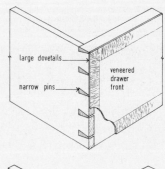

19. Charles II period lacquered cabinet on carved and silvered stand.

Fig. 5. Veneer cut away to show common dovetailing.

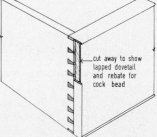

Fig. 6. Lapped dovetail and cock beading.

Veneers were sawn to the thickness of about one-sixteenth of an inch by sawyers who went from shop to shop for the purpose. Veneers sawn from the same log repeated its figure, and successive sections of the same pattern, matched, opposed or reversed, could be laid on the carcase—across for instance, a drawer front, or on the top of a table, or from top to bottom of a chest of drawers. On large surfaces, 'quartering' (laying four veneers with the figure twice reversed) was common.

The joiners' technique of panel and frame construction did not give the flush surface that was essential for veneering, and oak was an unsuitable background for veneers, yellow deal being both more stable and cheaper. Oak, however, was used for drawer linings in veneered furniture.

The most skilled craftsmen used veneers of rich figure, or cuts taken transversely from small branches of trees (which produced oval patterns known as oyster pieces), or burr veneers which were cut from malformations on tree trunks and produced, not a regular pattern, but a tangled mass of veins. These burr veneers were difficult to cut and apply, as they tended to curl, but they gave a most attractive decoration (Plate 48). As well as walnut, other woods, if they had an interesting figure, were much sought after for veneers by cabinet-makers, such as maple, yew, elm, ash, mulberry and kingwood, and, for oyster pieces, olive and laburnum.

The decorative effect of veneered furniture was enhanced in several ways. Cross-banded borders—i.e., short strips of veneer in which the grain ran across the width (Fig. 4), with a narrow inner 'herring-bone' banding, so called because it was composed of tiny strips of veneer of contrasted colours on the slant—were generally used on larger surfaces. Drawer fronts, however, often had herring-bone banding only.

The through or common dovetail which was used on early veneered furniture exposed the end-grain and did not give a satisfactory surface for veneers; it was therefore replaced by the 'lapped' or 'stopped' dovetail, which left a lap on the pin piece (Figs. 5, 6).

Closely allied to the technique of veneering was that of marquetry, which employed veneers of

20. *Left:* Interior of lacquered cabinet showing drawer space for the collection of 'curiosities'.

21. *Above:* Chased metal hinges, corner mounts and lock-plate of lacquered cabinet; these mounts were widely copied on contemporary walnut cabinets.

coloured woods to form intricate patterns (Plates 17, 18). The required design was first drawn on paper and pricked through on to other sheets to get duplicates. The pattern was pasted on top of several layers of veneer, which were fastened with panel pins or glued together with interleaved sheets of paper. The marquetry-cutter then cut through the whole of the veneers with a fine frame saw, along the lines of the drawing. Selected pieces of the design were arranged on the veneer ground in the manner of a jig-saw puzzle.

For floral marquetry, which was fashionable until *c*.1690 (and later than 1690 on clock cases), many woods were used, suitable shades being obtained where necessary by staining, dyeing, or scorching the veneers with hot sand. But after *c*.1690 arabesque or 'seaweed' marquetry became fashionable, and for this only two woods were necessary to give the contrasted light and dark shades —walnut for the ground and either box or holly for the pattern (Plate 29). A simple geometrical type of marquetry known as parquetry was composed of a ground of oyster pieces in narrow lines of holly, box or sycamore forming circles, stars, etc. (Plate 25).

Turning. In the early walnut period, spiral or twist turning of supports was one of its outstanding features, and for some years supplanted baluster forms (Plate 18). The lathe on which the turner had hitherto worked had only been able to cut shapes at right angles to the axis of the work, but a special device now enabled it to cut obliquely, so that spirals could be turned and then finished by hand. Sometimes a double twist was made, the hollows being completely gouged out to give an open effect.

In the last quarter of the 17th century baluster turning returned to favour, and some graceful shapes were produced in William and Mary's reign, particularly 'bells' and 'pegs' (Plate 26). But after 1700 turning declined until the advent of Adam's neo-classic style of *c*.1760 (Plate 67).

Mouldings. Mouldings—the projecting bands shaped by the moulding plane to the required section —added decorative effect to cornices, friezes, plinths, edges of tables, etc., and to fronts of chests of drawers. They were covered with cross-grain veneer. Tall pieces of the later Stuart period, such as chests on stands and tallboys, were given architectural style cornices by the addition of mouldings to

22. Walnut armchair with twist-turned supports, caned seat and back, and carved royal arms, cupids and crowns. Dated 20th February, 1687/8, and inscribed 'George Lewis' (i.e., George, Elector of Hanover, later George I of England).

23. Turned walnut 'sleeping' chair with adjustable back and contemporary upholstery; c.1670.

24. Oak chest of drawers on stand with baluster legs; c.1690.

form either a cavetto (i.e., concave) or a swell frieze. Various mouldings were found on chests of drawers. A half round moulding was applied to the carcase surrounding the drawer front after c.1690 (Fig. 7). This was followed by the double half round moulding between 1700 and 1715 (Fig. 8). After 1710 the moulding was fixed to the edge of the drawer and projected in ovolo section to hide the line between opening and drawer when the latter was closed (Fig. 9).

Lacquer and Japanning. After 1660 much richly-coloured lacquer furniture from China and Japan was imported into England by the East India Company, including screens and panels, which were made up into pieces of furniture, and cabinets, which were mounted on carved and gilt or silvered stands (Plates 19, 20, 21). Oriental lacquer (made from the sap of the lac-tree which was not found in Europe) became so fashionable that English furniture was exported to the East to be lacquered and brought back again.

This fashion encouraged an English imitation known as japanning. Enthusiastic amateurs japanned their own furniture, particularly after the publication in 1688 of a manual, Stalker and Parker's *Treatise of Japanning and Varnishing*, while professional japanners, faced with the competition of oriental work, successfully petitioned Parliament in 1700 to curtail imports by the imposition of crippling tariffs.

For japanning, the wood was given a coating of whiting and size, and then covered with coats of coloured varnish to form the ground. The design was painted on in gilding and in colours mixed with gum-arabic. Details in relief were formed by adding a paste of gum-arabic and whiting which was coloured and gilded. A form of incised oriental lacquer known as 'Bantam work' was imitated by japanners by cutting out the design from the ground of whiting and size, then colouring and gilding

25. Chest with lift-up top and drawers
below, on stand with twist-turned legs
and shaped stretchers; upper stage
decorated with parquetry of laburnum
oyster pieces; *c*.1690.

26. Walnut settee with turned
baluster ('bell') legs and waved
stretchers; contemporary
upholstery; *c*.1690.

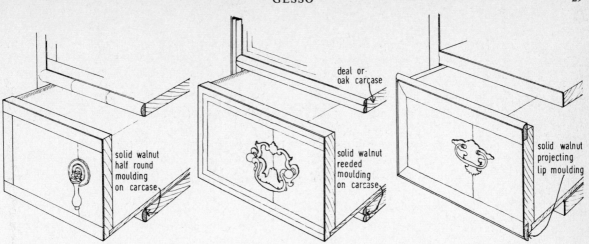

Fig. 7. Half-round moulding. Fig. 8. Double half-round (reeded) moulding. Fig. 9. Ovolo lip moulding.

it. Although many pieces of furniture, including cabinets, bureaux, bookcases and mirrors, were japanned with pseudo-oriental motives, English japanning was inferior to oriental lacquer both in colour and the vitality of the designs.

Gesso. Gilt gesso furniture became fashionable under Charles II and reached its peak from 1700 to 1730. Gold leaf was applied by either water-gilding or oil-gilding to a ground of gesso, a composition of whiting and size which was laid on the wood (usually deal) in several coats and left hard and smooth. For water-gilding the gesso was covered with a special clay and wet thoroughly; the leaf had to be applied with great skill and speed, as the water dried rapidly. A second coat of gold could be applied for fine quality work, and brightly burnished.

Neither this 'double-gilding' nor burnishing was obtainable by oil-gilding, a slower, cheaper and more durable method which was commonly used after 1660. The raised decoration found on the gilt chairs, mirrors (Plate 27), side tables, picture-frames, stands and cabinets of this time was first carved in wood then glued to the surface before the composition was applied. Armorial bearings and monograms were often used in gesso work.

The Early Walnut Period: 1660-90

The Restoration of Charles II in 1660 was an important landmark in English furniture history. Inspired by the example of the king and his court, who had become used to the elegance of continental furniture and decoration during their eleven years' exile abroad, the English upper classes sought more comfort and luxury. The rebuilding of London after the Great Fire of 1666 provided a unique opportunity to stock the new houses with furniture of the latest fashion. After eleven years of Puritan domination there was an understandable swing to elaborate decoration. The famous diaries of John Evelyn and Samuel Pepys make frequent reference to luxurious living and to new and varied types of furniture.

Typical of this period were the tall-backed walnut chairs with caned seats and back panels. At first legs, stretchers and uprights were twist turned; later arms and legs were scrolled (though they did not supersede twist turning in Charles's reign). Elaborate carving decorated the cresting rails and front stretchers (which had matching motives), and the back panel frames (Plate 22). Cane was widely used on chairs as it made them lighter. Daybeds or couches, with six or more legs, had similar decoration. Stools were still widely used and followed contemporary chair styles. Upholstered armchairs and settees with wings and padded arms, covered with rich imported materials like velvet and damask, or with wool needlework on canvas, worked at home, were introduced at this time (Plate 23).

Eating-rooms now had gate-legged tables, sometimes in sets of three, two of semicircular form being joined to a central rectangular one as required. Small tables with twist turned legs united by flat stretchers (Plate 18) were used about the house for a variety of purposes, a fashionable combination being a side table with a portable candle-stand at each side, and a mirror above. As mirrors were made at Vauxhall shortly after 1660, and were no longer all imported, they came into more general use, though still expensive. These early English mirrors, with plates up to about forty-five inches in length, were mounted in broad rectangular frames of convex section decorated with veneers or marquetry (sometimes with tortoiseshell and ebony enrichments).

It was usual to mount case furniture, such as writing cabinets, cabinets, bureaux, chests and chests of drawers, on stands with twist turned (and, later, scrolled) legs (Plates 24, 25). Writing cabinets, or scrutoires, had a large fall-front. Cabinets, with folding doors, were intended to contain the valuable collections of 'curiosities' made by the rich. It was the craftsman who could make these fine cabinets and decorate them with marquetry on the doors (inside and out), and on the drawer fronts, who took the title of 'cabinet-maker'.

Another new piece was the long-case clock, in which the long pendulum greatly increased the accuracy of time-keeping and ushered in the golden age of English clock-making (Plates 17, 29, 33). The smaller bracket clocks, with handles to facilitate carriage from room to room, used the 'bob' pendulum. Domestic bookcases were also coming into fashion, the earliest recorded being those which Pepys commissioned in 1666. Beds grew higher as the height of rooms increased, and now had their wooden framework hidden by expensive materials.

27. *Opposite:* Three pieces of *c.*1725: a gilt gesso mirror; a small walnut bureau (two feet wide) with bracket feet; and a walnut chair of the Queen Anne type, with cabriole legs and claw-and-ball feet.

The Later Walnut Period

William and Mary, 1689–1702. More restrained decoration on furniture became apparent after the accession of William and Mary, partly through the influence of the court and its Dutch cabinet-makers, partly through the inclination of English craftsmen, once they had assimilated foreign techniques, to avoid excessive ornament. Characteristic of the change were the new versions of marquetry in quiet buffs and browns or arabesques in two shades of light and dark, and the graceful baluster turning.

In addition to spiral twist and baluster, the legs of furniture were also of scroll, square (and tapering), and cabriole form. These early cabriole legs—adaptations of a quadruped's leg and hoofed feet—were narrow and still required stretchers, but they were to lead to radical changes in the next reign. Many kinds of feet were found, including hoof, bun, ball, and scroll. Often tenoned into blocks just above the feet were flat, serpentine stretchers which were of X shape, crossing directly and tied in the centre with a finial, or joined to a central platform.

Many chairs had tall and slender backs, which were shaped to fit the sitter's body, and were sloped backwards to a marked degree. The arched cresting rested above the turned uprights which enclosed finely meshed cane. The legs were often of baluster shape. An exceptional type of chair, in the style of Daniel Marot (a French Huguenot who entered the service of William and had a great influence on interior decoration) had rich pierced carving in the space between the uprights, and an ornate cresting which was duplicated on the front stretcher. Upholstered chairs without arms, and

28. Early 18th-century walnut armchair, with four legs of cabriole form; contemporary needlework upholstery.

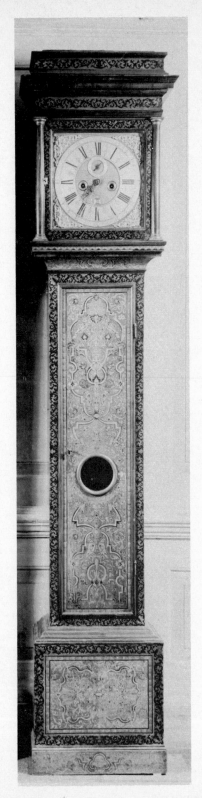

29. Early 18th-century long-case clock decorated with arabesque ('seaweed') marquetry. 30. Early 18th-century walnut secretaire-bookcase; the secretaire portion folds over.

31. A small Queen Anne walnut stool on four cabriole legs; c.1710.

wing armchairs, were becoming more common. Settees, of graceful form, had padded backs (Plate 26), wings and arms.

Tables specially designed for card playing, a fashionable craze throughout this period, had gate-legs to support their oval or circular tops. Other smaller kinds of tables included the writing table with rectangular top, and the dressing table with a knee-hole centre flanked by pedestals of small drawers (Plate 34).

The scrutoire remained a popular writing cabinet, and for greater stability was now supported on a chest of drawers. Its large fall-front, however, was inconvenient, and it was gradually replaced by the bureau with sloping front, which was at first mounted on a narrow stand with gate-legs to support the flap. Shortly before 1700 came the bureau on a chest of drawers, the flap now supported by brass elbow-jointed stays or by oak slides ('lopers') which pulled out from slots. Cabinets began to acquire arched pediments and sometimes had a chest of drawers for a base; a few had glass doors to display china. Chests of drawers with four rows of drawers were based on graceful stands having four to six legs (Plate 24).

Among the more ornamental pieces of this time were carved and gilded stands supporting lacquered cabinets, carved picture-frames obviously inspired by the naturalistic school of the famous wood-carver, Grinling Gibbons, and chimney glasses, the mirrors which extended above and across the chimney piece and had glass borders.

Queen Anne, 1702–14. Queen Anne's reign saw the production of some of the most attractive furniture ever made in England; simple, well-proportioned and dignified, it showed how far English craftsmanship and design had progressed since 1660. Graceful curves, beautifully figured and matching walnut veneers, and fine needlework are some of the distinguishing features.

Cabriole legs, now largely used on seat furniture (Plates 27, 31), tables and stands, marked a revolutionary change in construction, for they led to the discarding of stretchers, which went out of fashion for fifty years, until re-introduced on square legs shortly after 1750. They became wider and sturdier at the knees on seats when stretchers were removed, but achieved a slender and elegant form on tables. Great skill was required to make them as they had to be shaped and matched from carefully chosen lengths of walnut. Another well-designed feature was the angle bracket foot which supported case furniture at ground level and gradually replaced the bun and ball foot (Plate 27).

Chairs were excellent examples of controlled curves, with their hooped backs, vase-shaped splats of concave form at shoulder level, and cabriole legs, on which, about 1720, the celebrated claw-and-ball foot began to replace the earlier hoof and pad forms (Plate 27). Carving was mainly confined to

32. Early 18th-century mirror with flat veneered frame.

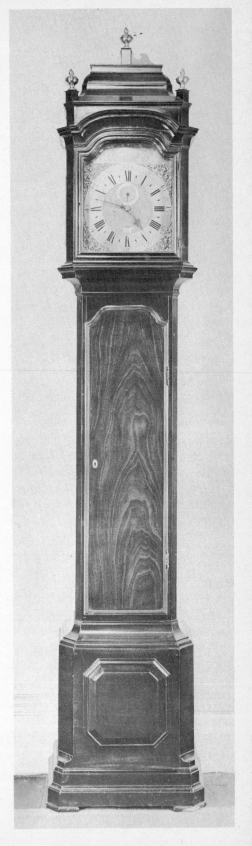

33. Long-case clock in Virginia walnut; movement by Daniel Delander; c.1725.

34. Early 18th-century walnut kneehole dressing table.

acanthus leaf or shell ornament on the knees, front seat rail and cresting. The more expensive chairs were veneered on the seat rails, splats and uprights, which were flattened for the purpose, and had four cabriole legs (unlike most chairs, which had the rear legs plain).

Settees now had lower backs and were of two main types: wide versions of upholstered chairs, or combinations of double chair form (which had been known in the early Stuart period). One version of upholstered settee for two persons has been given the modern name of 'love seat'.

Chests of drawers and bureaux acquired the forms which are still familiar and have never been bettered. One type of narrow chest of drawers (the so-called 'bachelor's chest') had a folding top for writing and seems to have been used in bedrooms. A popular piece of the early 18th century was the writing cabinet, then called 'desk and bookcase' (i.e., bureau-bookcase), the upper stage being usually faced with looking-glass plates. Many of these cabinets were of quite narrow width (under three feet), as also were bureaux and pedestal dressing tables, so that they could stand against the pier-wall—i.e., between windows, to get light from both sides. Although straight cornices were found on these bureau-bookcases, they often had arched domes and broken pediments, with gilt urn finials. Broken pediments, of straight or semicircular form, were so called from their central recess flanking a small plinth.

About 1710 the chest-on-chest or tallboy began to take the place of the chest on stand (Plate 36). The corners of the upper chest were often chamfered (as were sometimes those of the lower chest) and faced with pilasters headed by a capital.

Card tables, with slender legs, now had rectangular folding tops, which could be supported when opened on an extending leg. The top corners were rounded to hold candlesticks. One of the most charming of Queen Anne pieces was the dressing glass, a swing mirror on a shaped stand with tiers of drawers, which stood on the dressing table. Wall mirrors were tall and narrow and had flat frames (Plate 32) shaped at the top, sometimes with a central shell; they were often decorated with gesso (Plate 27).

35. Walnut chair with pierced splat and cabriole legs carved with coquillage; c.1735.

36. Walnut chest-on-chest (tallboy) with moulded corners; veneered with burr walnut; c.1740.

The Early Mahogany Period: *c.1725-55*

The second quarter of the 18th century produced two major developments—the introduction of mahogany and the entry of the architect into the field of furniture design. Mahogany, the most famous of all furniture woods, was already known in England, but its real introduction to English cabinet-making came towards the end of George I's reign (1714–27), when imports began slowly to increase after the abolition in 1721 of the high duties on West Indian timbers. No finer material could have been put into the hands of the celebrated Georgian craftsmen, whose great skill, stimulated by the demands of the wealthy and cultured upper classes, was to produce the golden age of English cabinet-making.

But mahogany took some time to supersede walnut, which remained in fashion until *c.1750* (Plate 48). Much walnut furniture of this time has been lost through attack by woodworm. The earliest kind of mahogany was the dark, heavy, straight-grained 'Spanish' wood from San Domingo and Jamaica, which was worked in the solid (Plates 37, 38). At the same time European walnut was largely replaced by Virginia walnut, a dark, unfigured wood also used in the solid. Thus from *c.1725* to 1750 mahogany and 'black' walnut were both employed by cabinet-makers (Plate 33). Much of this walnut was stained to imitate mahogany.

The fine qualities of mahogany were revealed as more supplies came from Cuba and Honduras. Its metallic strength encouraged experiments in design which had been impossible with other woods, and its great widths made it now unnecessary to join planks for table tops. Soon after 1750 beautifully figured wood was used extensively as a veneer, and could be laid on in larger sheets than had been normal with walnut. In addition, it had a fine patina, a wide range of colour, and resistance to warping and worm.

37. George II card table in San Domingo mahogany, *c.1745*; a good example of the texture and crisp carving of this early 'Spanish' wood.

38. Another example of early mahogany furniture — a gate-leg dining table in 'Spanish' mahogany, with unusual double-octagon top; *c.*1740.

39. Mahogany bureau; *c.*1740.

40. Mahogany armchair upholstered in needlework; legs carved with lion masks and paw feet; *c.*1740.

41. Mahogany mirror; broken pediment centring in a cartouche; frame carved with Vitruvian scroll; *c.*1745.

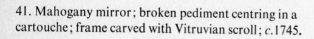

42. Mahogany side table with marble top;
carved acanthus and Vitruvian scroll ornament;
cabriole legs end on paw feet; *c*.1745.

43. Mahogany stool; legs carved with acanthus
leaf and cabochon ornament, and ending on pad
feet; *c*.1745.

Mahogany did not greatly affect taste at first. Early mahogany pieces are indistinguishable from their walnut counterparts. But the use of solid wood stimulated carving, hence the 'lion period' from *c*.1725–40 which took its name from the lion's paw feet and lion masks on the knees of cabriole legs (Plate 40), other motives being satyr masks, cabochons and shells, used with claw-and-ball feet. Chair backs began to lose their solid splats and took on an open design of narrow pierced verticals (Plate 35); chair arms often had eagles' head terminals.

Mahogany flap dining tables usually had four or six legs and oval or circular tops, and continued the gate-leg principle by having an extra swing leg on each side to support the flaps (Plate 38). In

44. Mahogany bureau-bookcase with broken pediment; *c*.1740.

45. Walnut and gilt chair; with pierced splat in form of shell, *c*.1745; showing transitional stage between early Georgian and Chippendale styles.

46. Mid-18th-century carved console table with marble top.

some of these tables an extra leaf could be inserted. By 1750 it was usual to build up long dining tables by fastening a semicircular pier table to each end of a centre gate-leg table with two rectangular flaps.

By 1750 also the new fashion for drinking tea greatly increased the demand for the tripod ('pillar and claw') tea table, which had three legs of cabriole form—the claws—dovetailed to the base of a turned pillar (Plate 47). Shortly after that date the top of the tripod table was made to tilt by being hinged to a small cage which was seated on the pillar and wedged to make it fast; the top could be lifted off when the wedge was removed. Square card tables with folding tops were sometimes given a hinged folding ('concertina') framework so that two legs could be extended to hold the flap.

For drawered furniture the cock bead, the most typical of Georgian mouldings, was introduced c.1730 and became universal from c.1745. This projecting moulding was rebated on the edge of the drawer (Fig. 6).

William Kent, 1685–1748. William Kent, artist, architect and landscape-gardener, was the first English architect to include furniture designs in his decorative schemes. Trained as an artist in Italy, and patronised by the cultured Earl of Burlington, he designed the contents of great houses in a monumental baroque style. His furniture—chairs, chests, bookcases, writing tables, pier glasses, 'terms and bustos' (i.e., busts on pedestals), 'marble tables' (i.e., side tables with Italian marble tops) (Plate 42), console tables (introduced from France and supported against the wall by two brackets (Plate 46) or a spread eagle)—was marked by elaborate carved and gilt decoration in soft-wood, or sometimes in mahogany parcel- (i.e., partly-) gilt. His ornaments included rich swags, human masks and figures, ringed lion heads and, on friezes, the Vitruvian scroll (or wave pattern) (Plates 41, 42) and Greek keys.

Kent's furniture was part of a unified scheme and looks ponderous when removed from its original position. It was conceived in architectural terms and had little influence on cabinet-making in general, though there was a short architectural phase in furniture in which larger cabinets, bookcases, etc., acquired classical architectural elements such as pediments (Plate 44), columns and pilasters, and cabinet-makers were urged to make a thorough study of architectural proportions.

47. Mahogany pillar and claw (tripod) table with finely carved feet and shaft; c.1745.

48. Bureau, c.1750, veneered with burr walnut—a striking example of the continued fashion for walnut. Made by Elizabeth Bell and Son.

49. Elizabeth Bell's trade label on walnut bureau (Plate 48). Very few Georgian pieces carried their maker's name. Elizabeth Bell continued her late husband's business from c.1750 in St Paul's Churchyard, for long the chief centre of furniture-making in London.

Thomas Chippendale (1718-79) and the Rococo Period

Recent research has revealed that among the outstanding cabinet-makers of the early and mid-Georgian periods were the partners John Gumley and James Moore, Benjamin Goodison, William Hallett, William Bradshaw, and the partners, William Vile and John Cobb. Yet the most famous name in popular (and international) estimation remains that of Thomas Chippendale, who has rather unfairly overshadowed his contemporaries, for although his workshop in St Martin's Lane, London, produced elegant furniture for fashionable clients, his was not the finest furniture of this time, and he did not gain a royal appointment. He is famous because in 1754 he launched a new style, the English version of the French rococo, in his pattern book, *A Gentleman and Cabinet-Maker's Director*, the first illustrated catalogue to be published by a cabinet-maker and to be devoted exclusively (in 160 plates) to furniture designs.

The rococo style was a revolt against formal classicism and was marked by a lively use of asymmetrical curves in C and S scrolls, in what Hogarth in 1753 called 'the serpentine line, or line of grace'. Chippendale also incorporated in his book designs for furniture in the Chinese and Gothic tastes, the former inspired by renewed interest in oriental styles, the latter by the Gothic decoration in Horace Walpole's house at Strawberry Hill. Chinese scroll work and figures, and Gothic tracery, blended harmoniously with the rococo, though Chippendale also used Chinese geometrical lattice and fretwork, and some furniture of this period was japanned.

The *Director* was intended to be a guide for craftsmen and wealthy clients. It was re-issued in 1755 and, enlarged to 200 plates, in 1762. Its designs were widely copied and freely adapted, and its success stimulated similar publications by craftsmen and designers. Thus Ince and Mayhew's *Universal System of Household Furniture* (1759–63) was largely based on the *Director*. One cannot,

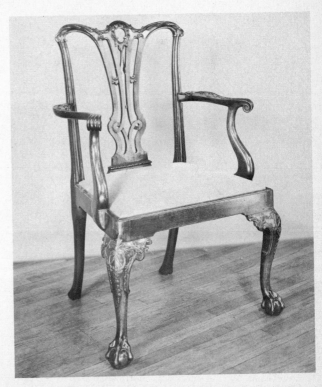

50. Mahogany armchair; cabriole legs and claw-and-ball feet; splat carved in the rococo taste; c.1755.

51. Mahogany armchair, with straight legs and stretchers; splat decorated with Gothic tracery; c.1755.

52. Console table finely carved and gilt in the rococo taste; c.1755.

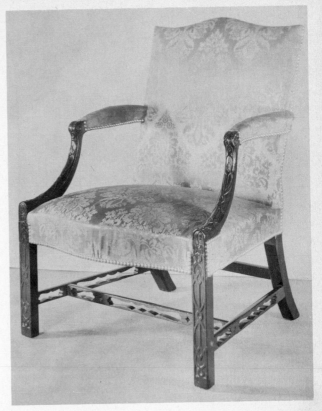

53. Mahogany upholstered armchair; arm supports and front legs carved with low relief lattice ornament; pierced stretchers; *c*.1760.

therefore, attribute to Chippendale (as used to be the case) the bulk of surviving furniture of this period in his *Director* style. Only a relatively few pieces can be proved to have come from his workshop, and some of the best of these were made later in his career, when the rococo style was outmoded. The best rococo furniture was made in Vile's workshop.

Characteristic rococo decoration can be seen on chairs (Plate 50), with their serpentine cresting rails, intertwined scrolled splats (sometimes in 'ribband back' form), cabriole legs, and French scroll feet (now replacing the claw-and-ball) (Plate 54); on commodes, the fashionable ornamental chests of drawers which stood prominently in reception rooms and closely followed French models with serpentine fronts and elaborate carvings; on console tables (Plate 52); and on carved and gilt mirror frames, some of which exhibited asymmetrical decoration in its most ornate form. These mirrors often had Chinese pagodas, bells, mandarins, birds, dragons, etc., mingled with scrolled foliage. Gothic motives appeared as arches and pinnacles on chair backs (Plate 51), glazing bars, etc.

The more extravagant *Director* designs do not seem to have been executed, for the traditional English instinct for moderation reasserted itself. Many chairs, for instance, had straight legs on which stretchers were re-introduced (Plate 51).

It was the great strength of mahogany which gave chair backs their daring scrolls and ribbons. The delicacy of the splats was enhanced by chiselling back and narrowing the reverse side of the scrolls, leaving the tool marks visible. Chinese chairs had large-scale lattice work backs (Plate 55) and, in some cases, pierced stretchers; their straight legs, generally square in section, often had a low-relief fret carved on their two outer faces, in the form known as card-cut ornament. The angles between legs and seat frames usually had a fret-cut bracket, the frames themselves sometimes having a strip of mahogany glued on, card-cut or pierced.

Library furniture received much attention in the *Director*. Since *c*.1745 the break-front bookcase (i.e., with projecting centre section) had come into use and continued to have architectural form with triangular or broken pediments. Open pedestal library tables were favoured, but no designs for

54. Mahogany armchair of the type described in Chippendale's *Director* as 'French'; *c*.1760.

55. Mahogany armchair; back filled with lattice work in the Chinese taste; *c*.1760

56. Mirror with carved and gilt foliage ornament; c.1755.

57. Chippendale period carved mahogany three-tier dumb waiter; c.1760.

D

58. Mahogany tea (or 'china') table; gallery pierced with lattice work in the Chinese taste; low relief carving on legs; pierced stretchers; c.1760.

dining tables were given, as these were still made up of separate units and were apparently of little interest to the designer. On the other hand, there were varied designs for writing, breakfast and tea (or 'china') tables (Plate 58). About 1760 the best pillar and claw tables had either a circular top bordered by a gallery or carved ornament, or a scalloped and raised ('piecrust') edge.

Bureau-bookcases had various elaborate designs and were intended to have glazed doors—a reversion to the tradition of the early part of the century. They were surmounted by a crested arch, swan-neck pediment or pierced fret gallery. China cabinets were appropriately given Chinese decoration, with a pierced frieze or pagoda roof.

59. Mahogany serpentine-fronted writing table with pull-out front section; scrolled brackets between legs and top; c.1760.

60. Mahogany serpentine-fronted chest of drawers; fluted and reeded canted corners.

61. An example of English devotion to French styles; an unusually early English version of a French *bonheur-du-jour*, with key pattern decoration; *c*.1760.

The Neo-Classical Period

Robert Adam (1728–92). In the 1760's the Chippendale style was replaced by Robert Adam's classical revival. Adam, the most famous of the Georgian architect-designers, was of Scottish origin and the second of four brothers who established an architectural firm in London shortly after 1758. Inspired by his studies of classical and Renaissance architecture in Dalmatia and Italy between 1754 and 1758, he developed the neo-classical style, a graceful and delicate version of classical forms and decoration. English furniture was to be immensely influenced by what Sir John Soane in 1812 called 'the electric power of this Revolution in Art'.

Some of Adam's furniture designs, which were 'invented for particular persons', were published in *The Works of Robert and James Adam*, the first part of which appeared in 1773. They were translated into practical, everyday furniture by George Hepplewhite's *Cabinet-Maker and Upholsterer's Guide* of 1788, a pattern book which showed the type of furniture generally made between 1775 and 1800.

Like Kent, but in much more detail, Adam planned the whole of the interior decoration and furnishing of his houses to conform to a unified pattern. Among his characteristic decorative motives were festoons of husks (Plate 69), vases, honeysuckle, paterae, rams' and satyrs' heads, and medallions, applied in a variety of ways—by painting, carving, fine inlay or in ormolu. Painting was usually carried out directly on beech, but it was also done on harewood and satinwood veneers in the form of festoons, borders and medallions, and sometimes copper panels or suitably shaped pieces of paper (Plates 70, 71) were first painted and then inserted into or glued on the furniture. Fine inlay is the name given to the marquetry of classical decoration now revived by Adam, to distinguish it from the marquetry of the Stuart period; the techniques of cutting and application were the same. By 1800 painted furniture had become so popular that it had largely superseded marquetry.

62. Mahogany serpentine card table; *c*.1765.

63. Large gilt settee in the French taste; *c*.1770.

64. Mahogany Pembroke table, with serpentine ends to flaps; fluted and tapered legs; inlaid paterae above legs; *c*.1770.

65. Mahogany armchair of *bergère* type with caned
back; decorated with carved fluting and paterae;
c 1775.

66. Mahogany bureau, with
inlaid decoration on flap in
form of ribbon; *c*.1770.

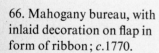

67. Mahogany 'spider leg' gate-leg table with slender turned legs; c.1765.

68. Serpentine-fronted commode decorated with marquetry in the French taste; c.1780.

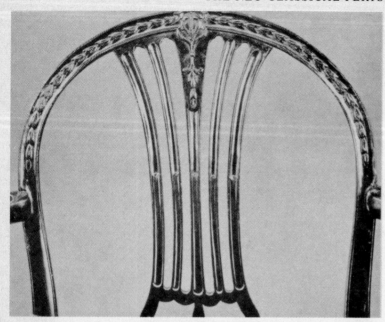

69. Chair in neo-classical taste; carved husk decoration of back centres in honeysuckle on middle rib of splat; c.1775.

70. Triangular corner table, carved and gilded; with painted decoration on frieze, top and stretcher platform in neo-classical taste.

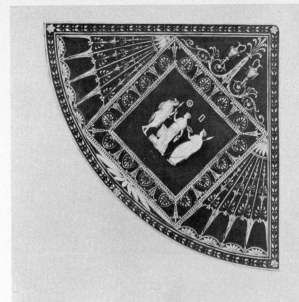

71. *Above:* The delicacy of Adam period decoration is well illustrated in this detail of the top of the table in plate 70, painted in black and white on paper.

72. Mahogany armchair of *c.*1775 based on French models—a concession to the influence exercised by France on the English upper classes.

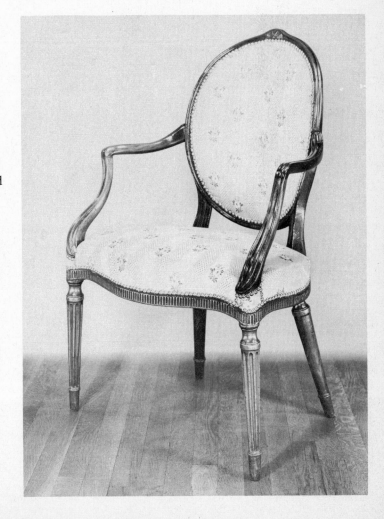

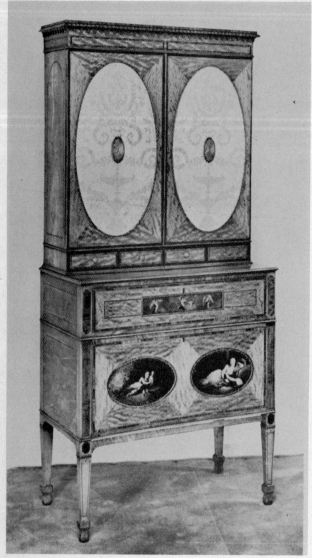

73. Satinwood bureau-bookcase of *c*.1780, decorated with carved frieze, inlay and painted panels; drawer front in lower stage lets down to form writing top; cupboard door lets down to disclose four central drawers flanked by recesses for books; oval panels in upper stage filled with patterned material.

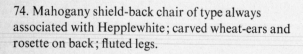

74. Mahogany shield-back chair of type always associated with Hepplewhite; carved wheat-ears and rosette on back; fluted legs.

75. Window seat painted with floral sprays and medallions, *c.*1790. Painted and japanned decoration was popularised by Robert Adam and Hepplewhite.

Bright ormolu mounts of classical design were used to great effect on a dark mahogany background. Ormolu is the term for fire-gilt bronze and brass; the metal, after chasing, was first coated with an amalgam of gold and mercury, then fired at a high temperature. This caused the mercury to evaporate and the gold to adhere to the metal, which could be brightly burnished. Ormolu mounts, formerly imported from France, were made for the first time in England by Matthew Boulton from 1762.

French influence is apparent in Adam's upholstered chairs, which had oval backs (Plate 72) and taper-turned or serpentine front legs, the latter ending on scroll feet. His neo-classical chairs had round or oval (Plate 69) or rectilinear (some lyre-shaped) backs; their legs were usually of square tapering form and decorated with fluting which ended above a solid plinth; oval or circular paterae were often carved on the level of the seat rail. Small semicircular side tables, commodes, cabinets, mirrors and stands were other favourite pieces for classical decoration. A novel combination of a side table and two flanking pedestal cupboards, each surmounted by an urn, was the precursor of the modern sideboard.

After *c.*1765 the attractive Pembroke table (Plates 64, 86, 88) in mahogany or satinwood became fashionable. It had obvious links with the older double flap gate-leg table, and had an oval or rectangular top; the central (fixed) portion was larger than that of the earlier tables as the two flaps were now supported by wooden (usually beech) brackets attached by wooden hinges to the framework.

Much of Adam's furniture was decorated with veneers of West Indian and Guiana satinwood (Plate 73), of which the light yellow tone enhanced the delicacy of his designs, especially against the pastel shades which he favoured for the walls of his rooms. The last part of the century is sometimes called 'the age of satinwood'. Adam's clients contracted with several leading cabinet-makers to execute his designs; among them was Chippendale, whose finest authenticated pieces were made for Adam's houses.

76. Mahogany armchair, centre splat headed by
three plumes. The number of designs of chairs with
square backs was increased in the third edition (1794) of
Hepplewhite's *Guide* to compete with Sheraton's
Drawing Book (1791–4).

77. Mahogany serpentine-fronted sideboard with
fluted legs and carved paterae on the frieze; *c.*1780.

George Hepplewhite (d.1786). As stated in its preface, Hepplewhite's *Guide*, with some 300 plates, 'designedly followed the latest or most prevailing fashion only', thus avowing its aim of popularising Adam's neo-classical style. Although it was an important and successful book (second edition, 1789; third edition, revised, 1794), very little is known about Hepplewhite himself. After apprenticeship to Gillow of Lancaster, he came to London and had a business in Cripplegate, but no furniture from his workshop has ever been identified. The *Guide* was published by his widow two years after his death, and it has never been determined how many of the designs were Hepplewhite's own or were those of collaborators.

Nevertheless, the *Guide* is a landmark in English furniture history for its skilful adaptation of Adam's designs into light and elegant furniture, free from exaggerated ornament, and intended to be made in mahogany and satinwood, or painted (Plate 75) or japanned. The many surviving graceful pieces of his period illustrate the fine standard of English craftsmanship and the excellent quality of the woods used.

The most famous of Hepplewhite's chair designs is the shield-back, which he developed but did not originate (Plate 74). He also used oval and heart shapes. Most of these chair backs did not have the splat connected with the seat but were supported as a framework by the upward prolongation of the back legs. Their decoration was carved or, if they were intended for drawing-rooms and bedrooms, painted or japanned. On carved chairs the frame was channelled (i.e., slightly sunk) and embellished with motives in neo-classical taste—vases, honeysuckle, festoons of husks, etc., and also draperies, wheatears and foliage. A novelty was the Prince of Wales's feathers, which Hepplewhite may have invented.

Usually chair legs were of square section, tapering slightly to plinth feet. The supports for chair arms now swept back from just above the front legs and up to the arms, which joined the back about half way up. In contrast, Hepplewhite also designed backs of square form, filled with rows of vertical bars (Plate 76).

78. Mahogany library table decorated with enamel plaques on the drawers; this table resembles a type illustrated in Hepplewhite's *Guide; c.*1785.

79. Mahogany cabinet; upper stage has inlaid floral decoration and Gothic glazing bars; c.1780.

80. Break-front bookcase in brilliantly-figured mahogany, with inlaid floral decoration and paterae; glazing bars in the Gothic taste; c.1780.

Few pieces of English furniture are more attractive than Hepplewhite chests of drawers and sideboards. Bow- and serpentine-fronted chests of drawers usually had the shaped drawer fronts of pine veneered with mahogany; straight-fronted chests were of solid mahogany, or of figured mahogany veneered on pine, oak or Honduras mahogany. From *c.*1770 the plinth at the base was discarded and, following French examples, the corners were carried down to the floor to outward curving feet (which replaced bracket feet, or short cabriole legs). A curved apron piece ran across the bottom of the frame. Drawer linings were of oak. After 1775 the bottom of large drawers was formed of two panels with a central bearer; this prevented the loaded drawer from sagging as it ran on its side runners.

Sideboards were of two kinds. One, developed from Adam's arrangement, had the former flanking pedestals and urns now fitted directly to the table. The other had square tapered (or, later, turned) legs at each end (arranged in sets of two at the front and one or two at the back) enclosing a drawer or cupboard; the front was generally of bow or serpentine form (Plate 77). Smaller sideboards, usually bow-fronted, and with four legs only, date from *c.*1780; a little later a tambour front sometimes enclosed a shelf beneath the central drawer.

Numerous varieties of small card, Pembroke and pier tables, on square or round tapering legs, were made at this time, generally of mahogany, sometimes with their tops inlaid or painted. Mahogany library tables adhered to the pedestal design, with neo-classical decoration (Plate 78). Wardrobes had a lower stage of (usually) four drawers on bracket feet, and an upper stage enclosed by two doors which often had veneers of Cuban mahogany 'curls' framed in a moulding. From *c.*1780 to 1800 semicircular commodes were in fashion.

The thin mahogany glazing bars on the glass doors of cabinets, bureau-bookcases and bookcases displayed graceful patterns (Plates 79, 80). Bed posts were also of particularly graceful proportions, and were turned and reeded, and carved with classical designs.

81. Mahogany armchair in the French taste; *c.*1780.

The Influence of Thomas Sheraton: 1751-1806

Sheraton's pattern book, *The Cabinet-Maker's and Upholsterer's Drawing Book* (1791–94), reflects the last phase of the neo-classical style and the culmination of the trend towards light and delicate furniture which had been apparent since the 1760's. It seems that Sheraton had no workshop of his own, and made no furniture, but his excellent designs reveal an original and discerning mind. The simplicity of his furniture is further explained by the need for economy during the French wars of 1793–1815, when the expensive processes of marquetry and carving were gradually superseded by the cheaper and more durable methods of painting and stringing (i.e., inlay in narrow lines) in wood (Plate 85) or brass.

The more crowded living conditions in London, and the general interest of craftsmen in mechanical gadgets at this time of the Industrial Revolution, also stimulated the output of compact and ingeniously contrived furniture. Sheraton's later furniture designs (*Cabinet Dictionary*, 1803, and the unfinished *Encyclopaedia*, 1804–08) lacked the inspiration and feeling for style of his *Drawing Book*.

The most noteworthy feature of the chair designs in the latter are square or rectangular backs (Plate 82) with a variety of upright fillings, tapered and reeded legs, and bold, up-swept arms joining the back near the top. For cheapness and lightness, many chairs were made of beech and japanned or painted, and often had cane seats.

Some of the most attractive of Sheraton's pieces were the small tables (Plate 89) with slender tapered legs (many of them specially designed to be easily moved about by ladies) which were fitted for a number of purposes—toilet and dressing, writing, needlework, games, etc. A 'Screen Table', for instance, had a writing slide and, at the back, an adjustable screen to protect the sitter from the heat of the fire; a 'Harlequin Pembroke Table' had a nest of drawers and pigeon holes which came up from within the table when the flap was raised. The pillar and claw supports of small tables, candle stands and pole (or fire) screens had, after *c*.1790, claws of graceful concave form resting on tiny peg feet.

82. Two Sheraton period chairs showing the square backs in favour from the end of the 18th century.

83. Mahogany semicircular sideboard
probably made to fit into an alcove; *c*.1790.

84. Mahogany oval table on central
column supported by four reeded outward-
curving legs; *c*.1800.

Among the innovations of this time were the sliding cylindrical covers (Plate 90) used on bureaux
and bureau-bookcases instead of writing flaps (these covers were formed of segments of wood glued
together, or of strips of wood glued to a canvas or linen backing—'tambours'), and Carlton House
writing tables with a superstructure of drawers and cupboards along the sides and back of their tops
(Plate 95).

Sheraton's sideboards resembled Hepplewhite's (Plates 83, 85), and were normally straight-, bow-
or serpentine-fronted; one design, however, had a concave centre (to help the butler when serving at
meals), and another, a 'Side Board with Vase Knife Cases', had pedestal cupboards which were
screwed to the central table. A drawing-room commode shown by Sheraton had a bow-fronted
centre flanked by straight-fronted wings, and a total of four doors; a 'Lady's Dressing Commode'
was of similar design, but had drawers at the sides, one top drawer having a basin for washing, the
other being fitted for writing.

85. Mahogany bow-fronted sideboard with inlaid 'stringing' decoration; c.1790.

86. Sheraton period maplewood Pembroke table with semicircular flaps; c.1790.

Towards the end of the century chests of drawers tended to become taller, often with a wide frieze above the top drawer. Sheraton illustrated two (which he called 'dressing chests') with a shallow drawer fitted for writing. The front corners were finished with reeded pilasters, square or round, ending on short turned feet.

It is no exaggeration to consider the Sheraton period as marking the height of technical accomplishment in English cabinet-making, for delicacy, strength and utility are found combined to a greater degree in furniture then than at any other time.

87. Oval mahogany folding dining table with inlaid decoration; c.1785.

88. Pembroke table with rectangular flaps, decorated with veneers of burr yew and inlaid 'stringing'; c.1785.

Regency Furniture: c.1800-30

When applied to English furniture, the term 'Regency' covers a wider period than the political Regency of 1811–20. It is a descriptive label for the revived classicism which sprang from the archaeological study of antiquities, and aimed at copying or adapting to modern usage the furniture of ancient Egypt, Greece and Rome. This fashion for classical purity, already evident in France, was introduced into England by the architect, Henry Holland (d.1806). His refurnishing of Carlton House (from 1783) for the Prince of Wales showed strong French influences; and at Southill (from 1796) the furniture made under his direction or from his designs incorporated both the late Louis XVI style and the new classical details (which were based on drawings sent to him from Rome by his pupil, C. H. Tatham). The strictly archaeological approach to furniture was at first confined to leaders of taste, and in England was interpreted in a scholarly way by Thomas Hope in his *Household Furniture and Interior Decoration* (1807), a collection of drawings which the author, a wealthy and widely-travelled connoisseur, used as designs for the furniture of his London home. Some evidence of this new approach appeared in Sheraton's later works, but when it was taken up fully by cabinet-makers, as in George Smith's *A Collection of Designs for Household Furniture* (1808), it tended to become an incongruous mixture of styles.

The best Regency furniture, however, showed admirable proportions and fine craftsmanship. Emphasis was laid on unbroken surfaces and straight lines, for contemporary opinion considered that ancient furniture was 'almost universally distinguished by straight or angular lines'. Dark, glossy woods with striped figures were used to set off the bright brass (Plates 96, 99) now widely employed for inlay, trellis work, galleries, lion paw feet, lion mask handles, star-shaped bolt heads, and studs. Rosewood from Brazil was in great favour (Plates 96, 98); so too were suitable selections of mahogany,

89. Early 19th-century serpentine-fronted occasional table with semicircular ends; inlaid decoration on top.

90. Early 19th-century bureau with cylindrical top, veneered with amboyna wood.

91. Mahogany folding-top table with sphinx heads, legs of animal form and decoration in the Egyptian taste; *c*.1805.

92. *Left:* Armchair in the Egyptian taste, *c.*1805. The cross-framed front legs are typical of the Regency period. 93. *Right:* Regency mahogany armchair of classical form, with wide shoulder board, key pattern decoration on the cross-rail and 'sabre' front legs; *c.*1805.

calamander and zebra-wood. Many pieces of furniture were of low height (Plate 96), their angular lines accentuated by reeding, so that the wall above them could have plenty of space for pictures.

Graeco-Roman ornament was faithfully reproduced with a new precision, particularly the palmette and anthemion (i.e., conventionalised honeysuckle design). A special feature was the use of Egyptian motives inspired by Napoleon's expedition to Egypt in 1798 and by the report of his chief archaeologist, Denon, in 1802. In England, Nelson's victory at the Nile (1798) made the Egyptian revival a fashionable craze (Plates 91, 92), of which the chief popular symbols were Egyptian heads and feet, the lotus flower and bud, hieroglyphics, griffons, serpents and crocodiles.

'Grecian' chairs became fashionable, characterised by bold, simple outlines, wide shoulder boards and 'sabre' front legs (Plate 93), these last two features being often also found on other chairs of the time. Also popular was the sofa or couch, in either the classical form of curved head-end and short arm-rests, or with a continuous padded back joining two curved ends.

Two new types of table are particularly associated with the Regency period—the circular-top table on a pillar and claw or pedestal base; and the sofa table (Plates 99, 100), which developed from, though it did not supersede, the Pembroke table, and had a rectangular top with two end flaps. These sofa tables had either two trestle-type ends connected by a stretcher, or were supported by columns or a pedestal on a platform with outward curving feet. Smaller tables included 'quartetto' tables, or nests of four, ladies' work tables with pouches for sewing materials, and tables for writing, reading, games, etc. There was a return to fashion of longer dining tables of extending type, with pillar and claw supports (Plate 94); large round ones, however, were also made.

The lighter type of sideboard of the Hepplewhite and Sheraton periods gave way to the revived table and pedestal cupboards which Adam had introduced, or to a large side table with a brass gallery on top and a wine cooler beneath. In contrast, there were a number of small bookcases with glazed or wire trellis doors backed by material, and chiffoniers, low cupboards with book shelves. A well-known Regency piece was the convex mirror enclosed by a circular, hollow-moulded frame.

94. Extending mahogany dining table on turned supports with curved and reeded legs; *c*.1805. The Regency period saw the revival of the long dining table.

95. Mahogany 'Carlton House' table; turned tapered legs with reeded cappings; *c*.1795.

96. Dwarf rosewood bookcase surmounted by a brass gallery; brass enrichments at top and bottom of corner columns; carved lotus leaf on feet; *c*.1810.

97. Mahogany writing table; turned legs with spiral (rope) decoration; brass lion-headed handles; *c*.1810.

98. Rosewood games table; trestle type supports with curved feet and turned spindle fillings; *c*.1810.

99. Rosewood sofa table, inlaid with brass ornament on pedestal support with four curved legs; *c*.1810.

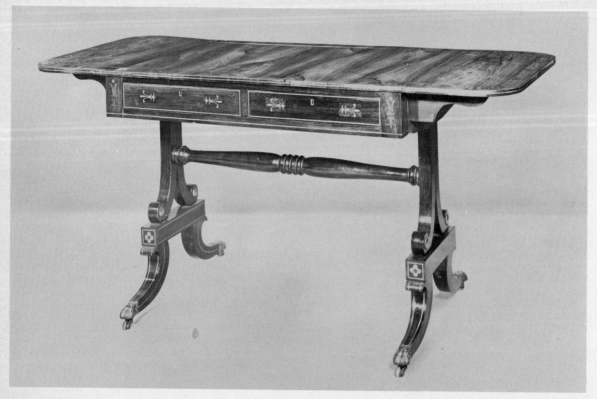

100. Another form of sofa table in rosewood, inlaid with brass ornament; trestle ends and curved legs with brass paw feet; *c*.1810. The sofa table developed from the Pembroke table and had a rectangular top with two end flaps.

The Victorian Period: 1837-1901

Victorian furniture has often been criticised, with much justification, for its poor design and ornate decoration. Rapid industrialisation and the great increase in the population led to a vast output of cheap furniture which, though it was not itself made by machinery to any appreciable extent until the end of Victoria's reign, was certainly influenced by the debased standard of many other machine-made articles, and was often characterised by hurried workmanship and shoddy materials. Even the best furniture, of good craftsmanship and materials, was often tastelessly elaborate. But recent research has led to considerable re-appraisal of Victorian furniture design. In particular, it is now recognised that the very ornate furniture at the Great Exhibition of 1851 was by no means typical, as many writers have supposed, of the period, but was, on the contrary, freely criticised by contemporaries for its showiness (Plate 101).

Moreover, much competent and interesting work was done by designers and architects (who increasingly turned their attention to furniture design), and by the end of the reign, under the inspiration of William Morris, there was a marked revival of good craftsmanship. Unfortunately, the work of these designers was too often debased by indiscriminate imitations by commercial firms who sought to catch the prevailing fashion without really understanding it.

Two important factors influenced Victorian furniture. One was the stress on comfort, for social life centred in the home and family. The rising standard of living and the rapid growth of cities gave more people than ever before the chance to rent or buy and furnish a home of their own. Cheap factory-produced textiles covered seat furniture with deep upholstery and tables with thick draperies so that the elegant framework of such furniture was lost. The second factor was the revival of historical styles, among which the Gothic predominated; this marked the end of classical supremacy and cleared the way for experimentation.

101. Design for a walnut and ebony carved cabinet by Freeman of Norwich, sent to the Great Exhibition of 1851.

102. Chair with upholstered seat and back panel, made of walnut. A style often described by Victorians as 'Elizabethan'.

103. Early Victorian sofa at Sheringham Hall, Norfolk. The deep buttoning so popular at this date can be seen here.

104. *Left:* Victorian mahogany balloon-back chair with upholstered seat, made by G. M. & H. J. Story of London Wall. 105. *Right:* 'Prie-dieu' or kneeling chair. Chairs of this design were popular throughout the early and mid-Victorian periods.

Early Victorian, 1837–60. In the thirty years after 1830 the standard of furniture design was particularly poor. Loudon's *Encyclopaedia* (1833)— its re-issue, practically unaltered, in several subsequent editions showed how much furniture lacked original ideas—named four prevailing styles: the Grecian (i.e., classical), Gothic, Elizabethan, and Louis XIV. But as art history was then in its infancy, the exact interpretation of these styles was by no means clear. Thus the Gothic and Elizabethan, both considered sturdy national styles, were frequently confused, and much 'Elizabethan' furniture was really reproduction of (often late) Stuart pieces (Plate 102). The Louis XIV or 'old French style' incorporated much of the Louis XV period and was inspired by the revival of *ancien régime* furniture in France after the Bourbon restoration of 1815.

Padded upholstery, which comfortably clothed chairs, sofas (Plate 103) and ottomans, influenced other types of furniture, for straight lines and rectangular shapes were abandoned for curves, rounded corners and semicircular plans. Wherever possible, surfaces were left plain and French polished, for inlay was out of fashion. Sideboards acquired mirror backboards, often three in number, with semicircular crests.

In spite of the confusion, this period produced two original chair designs. One was the balloon-back, which derived from both the Grecian chair with its broad shoulder board, and the scrolled Louis XIV type, until, between 1835 and 1850, the rail and uprights formed a continuous curve pinched at the waist by a cross-rail (Plate 104). The other was the 'prie-dieu', with a tall upholstered back and low seat and legs, which was clearly based on Charles II chairs but was at that time considered typically Tudor (Plate 105).

106. Early Victorian papier-mâché circular or loo table.

107. The Kenilworth Sideboard or Buffet (Warwick Castle), made by Cookes of Warwick, is one of the best known pieces produced by the Warwickshire carvers.

108. Oak table designed by Philip Webb; c.1870. Webb was the chief designer for William Morris's firm.

The early Victorians were fond of experimenting with a variety of materials besides wood for furniture. Some, like Derbyshire marble, had only limited success, but much furniture was made of metal, such as cast-iron chairs, benches and hall furniture, and iron and brass bedsteads, which were considered more hygienic than wooden ones and rapidly supplanted them. Italian marble was also widely used in bedrooms for washstand tops.

But the most popular of these materials today is papier-mâché, which was known in the 18th century and used for furniture from the 1820's. It was made in two ways, either by pasting sheets of paper on moulds, or by pressing paper pulp between dies. The result was a smooth, hard surface which was usually painted with floral decoration on a shining black background, or inlaid with mother-of-pearl (Plate 106). The amount of this furniture produced, however, has been exaggerated. Most of it was made by one firm, Jennens and Bettridge of Birmingham, and the papier-mâché was normally combined on furniture with structural members of wood or metal.

This period saw a revival of woodcarving, which was a dying craft during the Regency. A feature of some of the more elaborate pieces was their 'anecdotal' carving of scenes from popular romances and poems, or from local history or, on sideboards, of fruit and emblems of the chase. There were prominent schools of woodcarving in London, Tyneside and Warwick (Plate 107). Amateur enthusiasm was encouraged for the craft, aided by fret-carving machines in the home, and this, with the coming of machine carving, explains the mass of pseudo-medieval and Renaissance carving on much late Victorian furniture.

Late Victorian, 1860–1901. (a) WILLIAM MORRIS. Appalled by the ugliness of commercially-made articles, William Morris with some friends founded in 1861 the firm of Morris & Co. with the aim of making, by hand, artistic objects for home use, in accordance with his famous dictum, 'Have nothing in your house that you do not know to be useful or believe to be beautiful'. Morris himself does not seem to have designed furniture, but his firm employed, among others, the artist Ford Madox Brown and the architect Philip Webb to design simple workaday furniture, mainly in oak (Plate 108).

109. Wardrobe designed by Philip Webb, as a wedding present for William Morris. Door panels painted by Edward Burne-Jones in 1858.

110. Escritoire and stand made by Morris & Co. in 1893 and designed by George Jack. The marquetry is of sycamore and other woods.

111. Oak sideboard with carved boxwood panels and metal hinges, designed by Bruce Talbert and exhibited in the London Exhibition of 1873.

112. Dining room sideboard illustrated in *Hints on Household Taste*, by Charles L. Eastlake (1868).

In particular, the firm produced two famous chairs; one, which sold for five shillings, had turned ebonised beech frame and supports, and a rush seat adapted from a traditional Sussex country type; the other was an upholstered, adjustable arm-chair which attained great popularity in America as well as Britain. More ornamental 'state-furniture' was also made, mainly designed by Webb and painted by Morris, his friend Burne-Jones, and other artists of the Pre-Raphaelite school (Plate 109).

All this work was inspired by Morris's enthusiasm for the medieval period which he believed was unsurpassed for the skill of its craftsmen and their honesty of purpose. But c.1890 the character of the firm's furniture, though still of the highest quality, changed under the direction of the architect George Jack, who used mahogany and rosewood decorated with elaborate marquetry in the 18th century tradition (Plate 110), and of W. A. S. Benson, who incorporated a great deal of metalwork into his furniture.

Many of the firm's products proved too expensive for most homes, but Morris's ideals, forcefully expressed through his writings and speeches, were a powerful factor in checking the decay in standards of taste.

(b) ART FURNITURE. The period from the 1860's to the 1880's saw the 'art furniture' movement, a phrase loosely used to denote an emphasis on historical (mainly Gothic) styles. In spite of its abuse by manufacturers, this movement had much of interest and indeed of originality. It was launched by the publication of two designers, Bruce Talbert's *Gothic Forms Applied to Furniture* (1867) (Plate 111), and C. L. Eastlake's *Hints on Household Taste* (1868) (Plate 112). Their furniture aimed at a more practical Gothic style, emphasising rectangular lines and avoiding curves and ornate carving. Painting replaced carving as their accepted form of decoration.

The architect William Burges designed some highly original Gothic pieces based on his researches into medieval furniture, which he believed was all of simple sturdy form, covered with paintings (Plate 113). Burges was also one of the first to use Japanese motives, which were considered to reflect the same ideals as those of medieval England. But the chief interpreter of this Anglo-Japanese style, popular in the 1870's and 1880's, aided by the interest created by the opening-up of Japan by the West, was another architect, E. W. Godwin, who designed light and delicate furniture with slender supports which set a fashion in ebonised woods and forecast a return to simple, graceful lines (Plate 114).

113. Wash-stand designed by William Burges (1827–81) for his house in Melbury Road, London.

114. Coffee table and chair, both made of ebonised oak, designed by E. W. Godwin (1833–86).

115. Cabinet made in 1871 by Collinson and Locke, designed by T. E. Collcutt and made of ebonised mahogany with painted decoration.

116. Oak sideboard designed by W. R.
Lethaby, c.1900. The piece is lightly carved and
inlaid with ebony, sycamore and bleached
mahogany.

117. Oak cabinet, painted in red and gold,
designed by C. R. Ashbee and made by the Guild
of Handicraft in 1889.

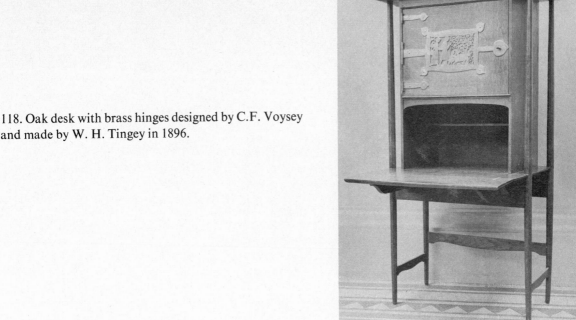

118. Oak desk with brass hinges designed by C.F. Voysey and made by W. H. Tingey in 1896.

Yet another prominent architect, T. E. Collcutt, designed a whole range of furniture for leading firms, from simple oak in the Webb spirit to detailed marquetry far removed from the medieval (Plate 115). He was particularly successful with dining-room chairs with two rows of small turned balusters on the back, above and below a central leather panel.

(c) THE ARTS AND CRAFTS MOVEMENT. Morris's influence was potently marked in the last twenty years of Victoria's reign in the Arts and Crafts Movement, which sprang from the formation of various guilds and societies of craftsmen and designers, mainly directed by architects, to combine social reform with the revival of good design and skilled, honest craftsmanship. The pioneer was the Century Guild of 1882 founded by A. H. Mackmurdo, followed by the Art Workers' Guild (1884), and the Arts and Crafts Exhibition Society and C. R. Ashbee's Guild and School of Handicraft (both 1888).

These societies spread their ideas through numerous exhibitions. Their furniture was by no means confined to the austere cottage-style joinery of the early Morris type, but, on the contrary, showed increasing interest in the 18th century (as evidenced by Morris & Co.'s later pieces) and moreover sometimes incorporated into furniture the work of other craftsmen (in stained glass, ivory, brass, etc.) (Plates 116, 117).

But Morris's ideas were most faithfully carried out, in design, techniques and workshop organisation, by the Cotswold School. This was an offshoot of the short-lived Kenton & Co. (1890–92), another Arts and Crafts Society formed by a group of architects, whose aim was to produce pieces of furniture each one of which was made entirely by one craftsman. Directly inspired by Morris, three members, Ernest Gimson and Sidney and Ernest Barnsley, set up a workshop near Cirencester in the Cotswolds in 1893. Gimson had already mastered the technique of chair-making through instruction from a Herefordshire chair-maker; now he concentrated on design, in close co-operation with his craftsmen. The result was the production of well-designed, beautifully-made and elegant furniture which, by keeping alive the best traditions of English rural craftsmanship, did more than anything else, as far as furniture is concerned, to hand Morris's ideas down to the 20th century.

119. Oak armchair and table, designed by Charles Rennie Mackintosh, c.1900.

(d) ART NOUVEAU. *Art Nouveau* was a short-lived, much-discussed but in many ways interesting phase which occurred at the end of Victoria's reign. As in many other instances, the style was so abused by the trade that though its inception owed much to English designers, by 1900 it was regarded as vulgar and foreign, and termed the 'Quaint Style'.

It began as a deliberate attempt to seek a new style for the 20th century. Among its general features were the continuation of the legs of chairs, tables, beds, sideboards, desks, etc., upwards, to end as free-standing columns with flat caps or, more rarely, under a moulding or cornice; a great deal of inlay in various materials, including stained glass; fretwork hearts and machine-made repoussé copper tulips (a favourite emblem of the style); the placing of stretchers on chairs and tables at just above floor level; and the incorporation of archaically-worded mottoes.

Some furniture of outstandingly individual character was designed, however, from 1893 by the architect, C. F. Voysey, who was regarded abroad as the fountainhead of *Art Nouveau* (Plate 118). Like the Arts and Crafts designers he used unstained and unpolished oak, but his own contributions were upward-continuing legs emphasising vertical lines, large door hinges ending in flat hearts, and chairs with thin, elegant uprights. Voysey's furniture was made mainly for individual clients in specially designed interiors which in their simplicity marked the first real break from the crowded and over-decorated Victorian rooms.

Some highly original furniture was also designed by the Glasgow architect, C. R. Mackintosh, particularly high-backed chairs, some as much as five feet tall. At that time, however, his furniture met with little appreciation in England, in spite of its welcome abroad as well as in Scotland, where it fitted admirably into its specially designed interiors (Plate 119).

The Twentieth Century

Up to 1920. The present century has seen the coming of the 'Modern Movement', which has slowly swept away Victorian historicism and done much to restore honesty and fitness of purpose to furniture design. It has meant an innovation of immense importance—the advent of the industrial designer, trained, with full awareness of the character of modern materials and methods, to design furniture of quality for large-scale production by machinery. This marks a technical revolution in furniture-making as far-reaching in its consequences as that of the panel and frame construction in the oak period, and of veneering in the walnut period.

Like these two great changes of the 15th and 17th centuries, machine art has reached England from abroad, this time from Germany and Scandinavia. It has by no means replaced hand craft, which has strongly maintained the traditions established by Gimson, who died in 1919. Thus the craftsman who produces single pieces, and the machine which makes a large number (with all the advantages of rapidity and cheapness) make up a complementary process of great value in the development of furniture, as long as the design and quality resulting from both methods are first rate. But the struggle to escape from the worst influences of the Victorian era and to establish sound principles of design, and above all to educate public taste to a proper understanding of machine art, has been long and difficult.

Until 1914 the exhibitions of the various members of the Arts and Crafts Movement continued to display furniture which illustrated the basic features of Morris's message—a thorough knowledge of materials and the setting and maintenance of the highest possible standard of craftsmanship in every detail. This furniture, and particularly that of Gimson, was among the most interesting then being made in Europe, and indeed received more attention abroad than at home, where it was appreciated by only a minority, most people being preoccupied with reproductions and the last phase of *Art Nouveau*.

120. Oak wardrobe designed by Ambrose Heal *c.*1900. Exhibited at Paris Exhibition. Inlaid with ivory and mother-of-pearl.

121. Chestnut wardrobe with one long drawer and interior all hanging space. Designed by Ambrose Heal, 1912.

122. Cherry wood and walnut bookcase. Designed by Ambrose Heal; c.1915.

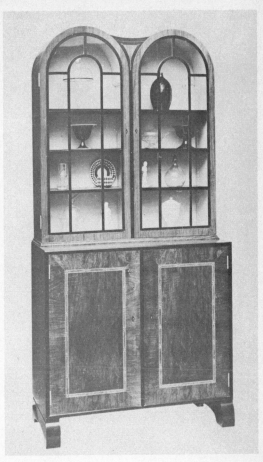

123. Cabinet of English walnut with ebony glazing bars and edgings; *c*.1922 (Heal).

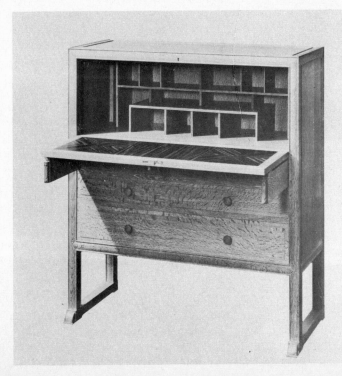

124. Weathered oak bureau designed by Ambrose Heal; *c*.1928.

125. Nursery dresser by Ambrose Heal, 1935.

The great mistake in Morris's teaching was his refusal to consider using machinery to make cheap and well-designed objects for everyday use. It was in Germany that the wider implications of his doctrine—that the ordinary man's house should be filled with pleasant things—were recognised in the foundation, in 1907, of the Werkbund, a group of architects, artists and manufacturers whose intention was to produce objects of high quality by machine as well as by hand; for, as was said at the inaugural address, 'it is not the machines in themselves that make work inferior, but our inability to use them properly'. The next stage in Germany was the establishment of the famous Bauhaus under Walter Gropius in 1919 to train 'furniture architects' to design for the machine, and this rapidly became the main centre of creative design in Europe.

In England the pioneer of commercially-produced furniture of good progressive design was Ambrose Heal (1872–1959), whose work in this field at this time ranks in value with Gimson's achievements in hand craft. Heal was reared in the Arts and Crafts Movement, whose principles he now carried into the furniture trade. Indicative of the new trends was the wardrobe he exhibited at the Paris Exhibition of 1900, with its plain surfaces of fumed and waxed oak and small inlaid panels of ivory and mother-of-pearl (Plate 120). But even more important than fine exhibition pieces has been the production by Heal's firm of simple pieces of good lines and fine materials for the ordinary market (Plates 121–125). As early as 1898 the firm's first catalogue of Plain Oak Furniture began the revival of simple wooden bedsteads of pleasant design which were to become very popular in the trade.

From 1920 to 1945. The lack in England of real experience of designing good furniture for machine production was clearly illustrated after the First World War. The immense building and furnishing boom of the 1920's encouraged the rapid output of furniture and almost complete use of mechanised processes. The design of this commercial furniture was, however, usually as poor as the materials

126. Fall-front writing cabinet in English oak
with solid burr oak panels. Designed by
Gordon Russell, 1921.

127. Chair in English oak; leather seat. Designed by
Gordon Russell, 1924.

128. Sideboard in English oak, with yew and ebony handles. Designed by Gordon Russell, 1924, and exhibited at Paris Exhibition.

129. Dressing table and chair in Australian walnut designed by Gordon Russell in 1928 to be made largely by machine.

Top: Library writing table (Osterley Park, Middlesex) and a Serpentine commode (The Lady Lever Art Gallery).

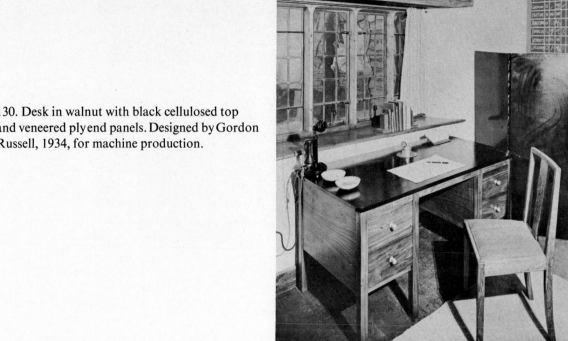

130. Desk in walnut with black cellulosed top and veneered plyend panels. Designed by Gordon Russell, 1934, for machine production.

with which it was made. The curious revival of pseudo-historical styles—Elizabethan, Jacobean, late Stuart, etc.—inspired such absurdities as the application of machine-made 'bulbs', carvings and mouldings to carcases, and it is possible that future generations will regard the furniture of these years as among the worst ever made in England. For 'traditional' was regarded merely as a spur to imitate the past, and not to design furniture in a straightforward way, with proper understanding of new materials and methods (as the great designers of the past had done).

Yet progress towards good design and craftsmanship has continued. Gordon Russell (b.1892) has provided the link between Gimson on the one hand and the continental 'furniture-architects' on the other (Plates 126–131). It is significant that he began his career as a designer at Broadway, Worcestershire, at about the time of Gimson's death, in the Arts and Crafts tradition, but has moved to designing also for machine production (Plates 129, 130). An important year was 1929, when the first of his radio cabinets for factory production showed a complete understanding of the nature of the problem and a triumphant solution. To have put a radio set in a 'reproduction' case would have been in the worst possible taste; instead, the advance now achieved in design, as successful as in the cases made by craftsmen (who faced a very similar problem) for the clocks of the late Stuart era, gave the best English radio cabinets a higher standard of design than anywhere else in the world.

The original Russell workshop at Broadway and the factory which has grown up behind it symbolise the joint triumph of hand and machine craft. Public interest was also aroused in the remarkable progress abroad in machine work, particularly in Scandinavia, where the Finnish architect, Alvar Aalto, designed some admirable furniture.

Meanwhile, at Petersfield, Hampshire, Edward Barnsley (b.1900), the son of Sidney Barnsley, Gimson's collaborator, established a small workshop on the Gimson model and produced furniture which clearly demonstrated that the finest traditions of the past were being fully maintained (Plates 132–135). An increasing number of small shops, including that of Peter Waals, formerly Gimson's foreman, and also the workshops at Heal's and Russell's, made similar furniture of high quality by hand.

131. Circular table and chairs
designed by W. H. Russell, 1950.

132. Bow-fronted chest of drawers in
figured black bean inlaid with holly.
Edward Barnsley, 1956.

The Second World War saw a unique experiment, the introduction of 'utility' furniture of standard specifications and designs necessitated by the shortage of timber and the loss of furniture through enemy action. A committee of eminent designers appointed by the Board of Trade drew up designs for the whole range of furniture, which were much better and simpler than had been common in the pre-war years. Although permanent control of this kind would hardly be desirable, and although the scheme did not perhaps meet the immediate success in the post-war years which its sponsors had hoped for (for many manufacturers reverted to period elaboration in their furniture, explaining that the public found 'utility' designs too plain), yet there is little doubt that the good proportions and clean lines of the well-designed furniture of the war period has had its effect.

The Post-War Scene. This increased interest in good furniture is very evident today. Hand craftsmanship of high order flourishes among a number of workshops throughout the country (Plate 136), of which Edward Barnsley's is still the best known. Their work is encouraged by such bodies as the Craft Centre and the Rural Industries Bureau. Craft work, taught by well-qualified teachers, is firmly established in the schools. A decided stimulus to the appreciation of machine work has come from the Council of Industrial Design and its permanent display at the Design Centre in London. A clear symptom of this interest has been the close attention paid in the post-war years to Danish factory-made furniture, which has achieved a great reputation for its skilful and attractive design.

Modern industry has produced machines for all the furniture-making processes, and materials for constructing furniture, which are quite different from the traditional ones. Woodworking machines have, in fact, a long history behind them, for in 1793 Sir Samuel Bentham took out an inclusive patent for machines for planing, sawing, moulding, etc. for large-scale work, and carving machines

133. China cabinet of rosewood inlaid with holly, Edward Barnsley, 1958.

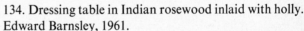

134. Dressing table in Indian rosewood inlaid with holly. Edward Barnsley, 1961.

135. Small sideboard in black bean, with tambour doors. Edward Barnsley.

136. Sideboard in solid English yew, with sliding tambour doors. Alan Peters.

were in use before the Great Exhibition, but these were very different from the precision furniture-making machines which are in use today. Veneers can be cut rapidly and cheaply by machine, either by peeling with a rotary cutter, which feeds a long knife into a revolving log after it has been steamed, or by slicing with a knife, in which case the logs are first sawn into flitches and then cut horizontally by the knife moving across the flitch or vertically by the knife moving nearer the flitch after each stroke.

Modern man-made timber materials have remarkable properties. Plywood is built up of uneven numbers of veneers glued together so that the grain of any ply is at right angles to that of adjacent plies. Blockboard consists of a core of wood strips about an inch wide sandwiched between veneers with their grain at right angles to that of the core. Laminboard is similar except that it has a core of thinner strips. Chipboard is composed of wood chips bonded under pressure with resin glues. All these materials have the great advantage over solid wood in that they do not split or warp; they are light and strong, ideal for large, unbroken surfaces, and can be veneered with selected timbers. Plywood in particular has immense strength, and can moreover be bent to curved shapes without damage, and even joined to metals by glues. One sheet of bent plywood can form the sides and bottom of a drawer, which is thus light and easy to clean.

Methods of steaming and bending timber also have a long history, for they were used by Michael Thonet in Germany in the 1830's. Recent developments in this line have produced structural members of great strength combined with lightness. It is possible, for example, to bend a single piece of prepared wood to form three sides of a rectangle and thus make the arm, front leg and support of each side of a chair, without the need of a back leg.

For jointing, machine-made dovetails are cut with revolving cutters which form both dovetails and pins in one operation on the two members to be jointed. Such dovetails show equal spacing of pin and dovetail, in contrast to hand-made joints, in which the pin is smaller than the dovetail. Very strong adhesives have been developed as a result of the use of plywoods, so that it is now possible to glue structural members together, such as a stretcher to a leg, without any other form of joint at all. Other types of fittings, developed from the modern use of metals, plastics and nylon, entirely eliminate the need for gluing, jointing and screwing, and are most useful for assembling unit furniture. There are constant improvements in plastics, and in cellulose finishes. All these materials are used by, and indeed serve to stimulate, competent designers.

Appendix I

GLOSSARY OF TECHNICAL AND DECORATIVE TERMS

Acanthus. Conventionalised leaf of classical architecture; much used as carved decoration on 17th- and especially 18th-century furniture (Plates 37, 43, 45).

Amorini. Cupids carved on Charles II chairs and other furniture after 1660 (Plate 22).

Anthemion. Ornament related to honeysuckle; more strictly, frieze with alternating honeysuckle and palmette (*q.v.*). Much used in Adam period, and with classical precision during Regency (Plates 69, 71).

Apron Piece. Ornamental rail connecting tops of legs on chairs and tables, and bracket feet on chests of drawers, etc. (Plates 40, 42).

Arabesque. Ornament of interwoven foliage, scroll work, geometric patterns, etc. (fanciful version of Islamic designs) used in 'seaweed' marquetry from *c.*1690, on gesso tables, *c.*1690–1730, and to some extent after 1760 (Plate 29).

Arcading. Series of arches on pillars carved on panels, especially in early 17th-century work (Plate 12).

Astragal. Small semicircular moulding often placed at junction of doors to keep out dust; or loosely descriptive of glazing bars of later Georgian period.

Back Stool. Chair without arms, as termed in 17th century.

Ball Foot. Spherical base of turned leg mainly in use in late 17th century (Plates 18, 25).

Baluster. Turned column, straight, spiral, vase-shaped, etc.; of particular interest on late 17th-century pieces (Plates 24, 26).

Banding. Decorative border on furniture in inlay or marquetry contrasting in colour or grain with main surface (e.g., satinwood with mahogany) (Plate 87); see also Herring-Bone Banding.

Baroque. Later (and more florid) version of Renaissance decoration seen in late Stuart carving and particularly in carved and gilt furniture of *c.*1725–50 by Kent and contemporaries (Plate 42).

Bead. Small moulding (*a*) of semicircular section on 18th-century furniture or (*b*) resembling string of beads. Bead and reel in combined round and oblong forms found as inlay in 16th century and in smaller forms in 18th.

Bentwood. Wood steamed and bent to form structural members of chairs, etc.; first developed by Thonet in Germany in early 19th century; taken up in England later, and widely developed in 20th century.

Blockboard. Modern furniture material composed of core of wood strips about one inch wide covered with fairly thick veneers.

Bolection Moulding. Ogee-shaped moulding projecting round edges of panels.

Bombé. French term for furniture with outward-swelling shape; applied particularly to English commodes in the French taste of the 18th century.

Boulle. Descriptive term for decorative inlay in metals and tortoiseshell carried out by celebrated French designer, A. C. Boulle (1642–1732). Practised in England by Gerreit Jensen at end of 17th century, and revived after 1815; 'seaweed' marquetry is a version of Boulle work.

Bracket Foot. Squared foot used from *c.*1690 on case furniture (Plates 27, 39).

Bulb. Swollen member of turned support on Elizabethan and Jacobean furniture, often with carved Ionic capital above, and with moulding of 'cup and cover' form; of Flemish origin (Plates 6, 10).

Bun Foot. Flattened ball foot introduced in late 17th century (Plate 26).

Cabochon. Convex oval ornament derived from gem; used in 16th and 17th centuries, and particularly *c.*1740 on knees of cabriole legs (Plate 43).

Cabriole Leg. Curved outwards at the knee and inwards at the foot; in general use *c.*1700–50 (Plates 27, 28, 35, 37).

Card-Cut. Ornament carved in low relief in lattice form, featured on 'Chinese' furniture of Chippendale period (Plate 53).

Cartouche. Tablet generally of oval shape with curled edges like a scroll, sometimes with inscription, arms, etc.; often found centred in broken pediments in early 18th century (Plate 41).

Caryatid. Support in form of sculptured female figure.

Cavetto. Concave moulding, quadrant of circle in profile, used prominently on cornices of furniture in walnut period (Plate 36).

Chamfer. Term for smoothed-off edge or bevelled angle (e.g., front edges of mahogany tallboys in 18th century); 'canted' and 'splayed' are similar terms (Plate 36).

Channelling. Grooves or fluting on stiles of oak furniture; also applied to grooved frames of backs of Hepplewhite period chairs (Plate 69).

Chequer. Geometrical inlay of light and dark woods found in oak furniture after *c*.1550 (Plate 9).

Chinoiserie. General term for decorative work in the Chinese taste, shown variously in japanning in 17th and 18th centuries, in Chippendale's 'Chinese' furniture, and in bamboo turning of late Georgian period.

Chipboard. Modern material made up of wood chips bonded under pressure with glues.

Chip Carving. Shallow ornament on oak furniture done with chisel and gouge (e.g., roundels on fronts of early chests) (Plate 1).

Claw-and-Ball Foot. Derived from oriental motive of dragon's claw clutching jewel or ball; celebrated terminal of early Georgian period (Plates 27, 37, 45, 50).

Club Foot. Resembling head of club; most common terminal of cabriole leg; used also with straight legs until late 18th century; when set on a disc, known as pad foot (Plates 28, 31, 43).

Cock Bead. Small astragal moulding projecting from edges of drawer fronts, much used 1730–1800 (Fig. 6, Plate 66).

Console. Bracket, normally of scroll shape; also applied to table (of French origin) supported against wall only at front by legs, or by eagle, etc., introduced in early 18th century (Plate 52).

Coquillage. Carved ornament of shell form used often in rococo period (Plates 27, 35).

Cornice. Top member of entablature—i.e., moulded projection surmounting frieze.

Cup and Cover. See Bulb.

Cupid's Bow. Term applied to curved cresting of chairs introduced *c*.1730 and prominent feature of Chippendale period (Plate 50).

Dentil. Moulding of small rectangular blocks ('teeth'), with spaces between, mainly used on cornices of mahogany furniture (Plates 79, 80).

Dolphin. Motive borrowed from France, first seen in late 17th century as terminal (arms and feet of chairs), then popularised by Kent and subsequently in Chippendale's rococo furniture.

Dowel. Wooden peg used in oak period to join timber.

Ebonised Wood. Stained black to imitate ebony; used for stringing in late Georgian period, and also for furniture in Anglo-Japanese style popularised by Godwin from *c*.1870 (Plate 114).

Egg and Dart. Classical decoration of alternating eggs and darts (said to symbolise life and death) usually carved on ovolo mouldings (Plate 41).

Egyptian Taste. Current after Napoleon's invasion of Egypt, 1798, and Nelson's victory at the Nile; manifested in sphinx head, lotus leaf, lion's head, etc., of Regency period (Plates 91, 92).

Escutcheon. Armorial shield forming centre of pediments of 18th-century furniture; also applied to ornamental metal plate surrounding keyhole.

Fielded Panel. With flat centre surrounded by bevelled edges.

Finial. Knob ornament (often vase-shaped) used on intersection of stretchers in late 17th century, and also on tops of cabinets, clock cases and pole screens (Plates 26, 33).

Fluting. Concave grooves used from 16th century onwards, but particularly on friezes and columns in late 18th century (Plates 47, 60, 64).

French Scroll. Leg terminal of outward scrolling form fashionable *c*.1750; opposite of inward turning knurl foot (Plates 54, 63).

Frets. Decorative patterns, either perforated (e.g., galleries of tea tables) or in solid (e.g., chair legs); fashionable on 'Chinese' furniture of Chippendale period.

Frieze. Horizontal section below table tops and cornices of cabinets, etc.

Gadrooning (Nulling). Carved repetitive edging of concave flutes or convex reeds, sometimes in S-form, used in oak period (e.g., on bulbs) and again from 1750 (Plate 10).

Gesso. Composition of parchment size and chalk used as base for gilding and (rarely) silvering; fashionable *c*.1690–1730 (Plate 27).

Greek Key (or Fret). See Key Pattern.

Griffin. Fabulous creature with eagle's head and wings and lion's body used occasionally as decoration on Georgian furniture.

Guilloche. Ornament of interlaced circles or ovals used on oak furniture from Elizabethan period and throughout 18th century (Plates 6, 12).

Herring-Bone Banding. Border of narrow bands of striped veneer laid obliquely together.

Hipping. Extension of cabriole leg upwards to join seat rail, found on chairs and settees *c*.1700–50 (Plate 27).

Hoof Foot. Terminal of early cabriole leg, introduced from continent in late 17th century.

Husks. Flowers strung as festoons; characteristic decoration in Adam and Hepplewhite period (Plate 69).

Key Pattern. Classical frieze ornament of repeated patterns of lines at right angles to one another, much used in Kent period (Plates 61, 93).

Knurl Foot. See French Scroll.

Laminboard. Similar to blockboard (*q.v.*) but with core of thinner strips.

Linenfold. Parchment or serviette pattern of Flemish origin used as panel decoration *c*.1480–1550.

Lion Mask. Carved decoration particularly on knees of cabriole legs *c*.1725–40 (hence the 'lion' period); revived during Regency in brass for drawer handles, as well as carved motive (Plates 40, 97).

Lotus. The 'water lily of the Nile'; fashionable decorative motive of the Egyptian taste during Regency (Plate 96).

Lozenge. Diamond-shaped panel decoration of Jacobean period (Plate 11).

Lunette. Decoration of half-moon form often found carved on later oak furniture, or inlaid and painted in Adam period (Plates 10, 11, 13).

Mitre. Intersection of moulding round panel, each edge cut at an angle of 45°.

Monopodium. Support of classical form for tables, etc., in shape of animal head and body with single leg and foot; fashionable during Regency.

Mortise. Cavity in wood to take corresponding projecting tenon to form joint (hence 'joined' furniture, joinery, joiner) (Fig. 2).

Neo-Classical. Term applied to revived classical decoration in delicate form associated with Robert Adam *c*.1760–90.

Ogee. Moulding of waved form, convex above, concave below.

Ormolu. Gilded metal used for furniture mounts; manufactured in England by Matthew Boulton from 1762 (Plate 59).

Ovolo. Convex moulding of quarter-circle section used on drawer fronts in late 17th century (Fig. 9).

Oyster Pieces. Small veneers of walnut, laburnum, olive, etc., cut transversely from branches and used in parquetry from 1660 (Plate 25).

Pad Foot. See Club Foot.

Palmette. Palm leaf ornament, similar to honeysuckle, like spread fan (Plate 71).

Papier-Mâché. Patent for version of this material taken out by Henry Clay in 1772 and used for furniture; but true papier-mâché furniture fashionable 1825–50 (Plate 106).

Parquetry. Geometrically-patterned veneers of oyster pieces (*q.v.*).

Patera. Round or oval disc decoration on furniture in the neo-classical style, carved, inlaid or painted (Plates 64, 65, 77).

Pediment. Classical triangular member surmounting cornices of cabinets, etc.; in use from 1660, but 'broken' pediments (straight, semicircular or swan-necked) popular in 18th century (Plates 41, 44).

Piecrust. Term for raised and scalloped edging of tea tables *c*.1750–75.

Pier. Part of room wall between windows; hence pier glass, pier table.

Pilaster. Flat column applied to cabinet, etc.

Pillar and Claw. Tripod composed of turned upright and three feet. (Plate 47).

Plinth. Foundation of carcase; plinth (or spade) foot of tapered rectangular form used in Hepple-white period (Plates 76, 85).

Plywood. Board built up from veneers glued together, each with grain at right angles to next, giving great strength (Plate 130).

Rebate. Rectangular channel on edge of framing or of drawer (e.g., for insertion of cock bead) (Fig. 6).

Reeding. Convex raised ornament (opposite of fluting) often found on chair and table legs, etc., in later Georgian period (Plates 84, 92).

Rococo. (French *rocaille*). Form of decoration succeeding Baroque and using C and S scrolls often asymmetrically in supposed imitation of rock work; English version of furniture in this style popularised in Chippendale's *Director* (1754) (Plates 50, 52).

Romayne Decoration. Medallioned heads in profile found on early Tudor furniture as attempt at Renaissance decoration (Plate 4).

Shell. See Coquillage.

Splat. Vertical member in centre of chair back, usually shaped or pierced (Plates 27, 50).

Split Baluster. Member turned, split and applied to furniture as decoration in first half of 17th century (Plates 10, 15).

Stile. Vertical section of frame of panel into which horizontal section (rail) fitted (Fig. 2).

Strapwork. Interlaced carved geometrical bands or straps (of Flemish origin) found on furniture from *c*.1550.

Stretcher. Bar uniting and bracing legs of chairs, tables, etc.; usually horizontal (Plate 51), but waved shape used in late 17th century (Plate 18).

Stringing. Inlay in fine lines often found on late Georgian furniture in brass and ebonised wood (Plates 85, 88).

Tambour. Shutter or roll front of desks, etc., formed of narrow strips of wood on canvas backing, introduced in late Georgian period.

Tenon. See Mortise.

Tester. Wooden canopy over bedstead (Plate 8).

Tudor Rose. Combination of red (Lancastrian) and white (Yorkist) roses used as carved decoration on early Tudor furniture.

Vitruvian Scroll. 'Wave' pattern of convoluted scrolls found on friezes of tables, etc., particularly in Kent period, *c*.1725–50 (Plates 41, 42).

Windsor Chair. Traditional country 'stick-back' chair (with no known connection with Windsor), often with frame of yew or ash, legs and spindles ('sticks') of beech, and seat of ash or elm. Early 'comb-back' type followed by 'hoop-back' after *c*.1750; simplified versions of fashionable details often added (e.g., cabriole legs, cupid's bow cresting). Manufacture of these chairs became organised in High Wycombe from early 19th century.

Appendix II

GLOSSARY OF WOODS

The following notes indicate briefly (a) the source of supply (if foreign), (b) the character of the wood, and (c) how and when the wood was used.

A. TO 1830

Acacia. Dull yellow, brown veins and markings; next to oak for durability; country work chiefly in 18th century as substitute for tulipwood, and for bandings and inlay.

Alder. White when first cut, then red, then flesh colour; country-made chairs, tables, etc., in 18th century.

Amboyna. West Indies; light warm brown with close figure (like thuya); surface veneers and inlays and bandings in 18th century.

Apple. Light warm reddish-brown; veneer and inlay in 17th century (and for long-case clocks); country work in 18th century.

Ash. White, yellowish-brown streaks, tough and hard but very subject to worm; after 1700 used for drawer linings, country pieces, and especially seats of Windsor chairs; some decorative veneers of knotted wood used (rarely) in late Georgian period.

Baywood. Mahogany (*q.v.*) from Bay of Honduras.

Beech. White to pale brown, readily subject to worm; continuous use from 1650 for cheap furniture and as substitute for walnut; sometimes stained to resemble mahogany; much used (owing to cheapness) for painted chairs of late Georgian period.

Birch. Light reddish brown, silvery streaks; country furniture in 18th century; suitable cuts used as substitute for satinwood after 1780. North American variety imported from 1750.

Boxwood. Central and southern Europe; light yellow, very dense and heavy (only European wood that sinks in water); inlay on oak from 16th century; used for lines on parquetry in late 17th century; inlay and border lines on satinwood, late 18th century.

Brazilwood. Brazil and West Indies; red, with rich colour after polish; inlay in 17th century; rarely used in 18th.

Burr wood. Malformations from trunk; inlays and veneers from 16th century, especially alder, elm, maple.

Calamander. Ceylon; light brown, striped with black; used for veneers and bandings in Sheraton and Regency periods; scarce by 1830.

Camphor. East Indies; soft yellowish brown; boxes and travelling trunks in late 18th century.

Cedar. North America, West Indies, Honduras; light reddish-brown; from 1750 for drawer linings, boxes, travelling chests, wardrobe trays. (Cedar of Lebanon *not* used in furniture.)

Cherry. Reddish, hard, close-grained; in use from medieval times; inlay in 17th century on oak and walnut; replaced by imported woods in Georgian period.

Chestnut. (*a*) Horse Chestnut; white; drawer linings. (*b*) Sweet (or Spanish), grown in England; light brown, white sapwood; used late 17th century for carved chairs resembling walnut. Both kinds, suitably figured, used as substitute for satinwood after 1750.

Coromandel, or Bombay Ebony. India; black, yellowish mottles or thin stripes; bandings in Sheraton and Regency periods.

Cypress. Persia and Levant; reddish, hard, very durable; used from 14th century for chests to resist worm and moth.

Deal. Scots pine, northern Europe; yellow or red; yellow deal used for carcase work (in place of oak) in walnut period; red deal carcases in use after 1750 as base for veneers. Red deal also imported from North America.

Dogwood. Light yellow sapwood, yellowish-red heart, very hard; inlays in 16th and 17th centuries.

Ebony. From the East; black, very hard and heavy; inlays in 16th and 17th centuries; inlays and veneers in 17th and 18th centuries. 'Ebonised' woods (i.e., stained to imitate ebony) largely replaced ebony by 1800 (*cf.* pear, willow).

Elm. Brown, tough and hard, but subject to worm and warping; country furniture in 18th century, particularly seats of Windsor chairs. Burr elm used as veneer in same period. Wych (Scotch) elm, with more figure, preferred for furniture since medieval times, but little has survived.

Fustic. West Indies; yellowish; inlays in 17th and 18th centuries, also veneers from 1750, but discarded by 1800 owing to its 'dead brownish hue' (Sheraton).

Harewood. Sycamore stained greenish-grey; bandings and veneers after 1750. Also called 'silverwood'.

Holly. Whitest of all hard woods; inlays on oak and walnut in 16th century; marquetry in late Stuart and Georgian periods.

Kingwood. Brazil; confused with rosewood, but of lighter colour; some (rare) use as veneer on late Stuart cabinet work, when also known as 'princes wood'; more frequently as cross-banded borders in late 18th century.

Laburnum. Yellowish, brown streaks, hard and durable; oyster pieces used as parquetry veneer after 1660.

Lignum Vitae. West Indies; dark brown with black streaks; intensely hard; used as oyster pieces in parquetry after 1660, and as veneer on small furniture in 18th century.

Lime. Pale yellow or white; soft and cuts well with or across grain—and thus the 'carver's wood', much used by Grinling Gibbons after 1660 and carvers generally.

Mahogany. (*a*) 'Spanish' mahogany (from San Domingo, Jamaica, Cuba and Puerto Rico), dense, dark, heavy and with little figure, chiefly used from beginning of regular trade in early 1720's until *c*.1750, mainly in the solid with carved enrichments. From 1750 Cuban variety more popular, as easier to work and often with fine figures, the best of which used for veneers. The strength of mahogany encouraged the revolutionary changes in chair splat designs in the Chippendale era. (*b*) Honduras mahogany ('baywood'), lighter in colour and weight, much used in later 18th century, often as carcase for Cuban veneers.

Maple. White; in marquetry (often stained) in 17th and 18th centuries, and sometimes as veneer. ('Bird's eye' variety of 19th century cut from American sugar maple.)

Oak. The premier wood until *c*.1660, and much later for country furniture. Bog oak (from peat bogs and therefore black) used as inlay in the 'oak period'.

Olive. Southern Europe; greenish-yellow, dark markings; used (as oyster pieces) for parquetry, and for cross-grain mouldings in late Stuart period; in 18th century some limited use as veneer, and also occasionally in the Regency period.

Padouk. Burma; red, hard and heavy, grain resembling rosewood; used (rarely) in solid (including chairs) *c*.1750; also for fretwork.

Partridge Wood. Brazil; heavy, with straight grain and streaks of brown and red resembling partridge feathers; inlay and parquetry in 17th century; occasionally as veneer in late 18th century.

Pear. Yellowish, tinged with red; smooth grain, unfigured; works well and sometimes used by carvers. Much used in country furniture; also for inlay in late oak period, for veneers on cabinet-work and clock cases in 17th century, and for picture frames in 17th and 18th centuries. Its close grain very suitable for staining to resemble ebony.

Pine. See Deal.

Plane. White, close-grained, tough; inlay and veneer in later 18th century, and for painted chairs (instead of beech) in country areas.

Plum. Yellow or reddish brown; heavy and hard; inlay and turning in 17th century.

Princes Wood. See Kingwood.

Purple Wood. Brazil; purple, turning to brown with age and resembling rosewood; hard and heavy; veneers and bandings from 1750.

Rosewood. India and Brazil; varies from deep brown to hazel, with dark streaks; heavy, dense and hard to work; used from 16th century as inlay; as veneer in 18th century; and frequently in solid during the Regency, its greatest period.

Sabicu. Central America, Cuba; hard and heavy, often similar to mahogany and rosewood; very occasional use as bandings from 1750, and (rarely) as veneer or in solid.

Satinwood. (*a*) West Indies and Guiana from *c*.1760 and (*b*) East Indies from *c*.1780. Both of yellow tone and of either plain grain or rich figure, but former variety has clearer grain under polish and used as veneer on fine furniture in Adam period (only rarely in solid). East Indian variety used widely until supplanted by rosewood after 1800.

Snakewood. Guiana and India; red heart wood, with dark mottled markings; inlay in 17th century, veneer in late Georgian period.

Sycamore. White, yellowing with age; fine grain taking good polish; also with rippled figure like varieties of satinwood and mahogany; used for floral marquetry after 1660, and also in solid and as veneer in satinwood period *c*.1765–90. (See also Harewood).

Teak. India, Burma, Ceylon; dark brown, straight-grained, oily; occasionally used in 18th century.

Thuya. Africa; warm brown, with 'bird's eye' pattern separated by wavy lines; veneers in late Stuart period, but often troublesome to lay.

Tulip Wood. Brazil; light brown with broad reddish stripes; veneers and cross-banded borders in Georgian period and especially Regency.

Walnut. (*a*) European variety in use from Tudor period, but mainly from *c*.1660–1750 as veneer (figured wood) or in solid (plain wood). (*b*) Black, or Virginia, walnut (also grown in England after 1650), greyish-brown with much dark marking, hard and dense, less liable to attack by worm; used mainly in solid in early 18th century.

Willow. White, soft, light; dyed black as substitute for ebony, in 17th and 18th centuries.

Yew. Reddish-brown, wavy figure and dark spots,

polishing well; in veneered furniture from 1660; in backs of Windsor chairs in 18th century; burr veneers similar to amboyna and substituted for it in 18th century.

Zebra-Wood. Guiana; light brown with strongly contrasted stripes of dark brown; hard, heavy, durable; veneer in late 18th century, generally as cross-banding; very scarce by 1820.

B. SINCE 1830

Since 1830 the extension of trade routes and especially the opening up of Africa have increased enormously the number of woods available for furniture, of which the following is a selected list. Some woods in section A are repeated here if their sources of supply have significantly changed, or they have been put to other uses, or they are of different varieties (but use the same name). Most of these modern woods are available as veneers.

Abura. Tropical Africa; light pinkish brown; easy to work, takes good finish.

Afara (Limba). Tropical Africa; light-yellow with greyish-black markings; easy to work.

African Walnut (Lovoa). Not true walnut, but related to mahogany; brown with dark streaks; veneer shows golden lustre.

Afrormosia. Ghana; brownish yellow, darker streaks; very strong and hard; resembles teak, but not oily.

Agba. Tropical Africa; yellowish to pink; fine texture, grain resembling mahogany.

Alder. Europe and U.S.A.; easily stained to resemble mahogany and walnut; also used for plywood cores.

Ash. Tough, strong wood; bends well when steamed, extensively used for furniture frames; also takes excellent polish.

Avodire. W. Africa; pale cream, darkens with age; fine satiny finish, but rather difficult to work and becoming rare.

Beech. Bends easily when steamed; much used for chair backs, etc.

Birch. Europe, N. America; strong and hard wearing, easy to work, takes good finish; bends easily when steamed. Much used for modern Scandinavian machine-made furniture (e.g., by Alvar Aalto, Finland); Finnish birch also widely used for plywood.

Black Bean. Australia; pale yellow to blackish, with broken lines of lighter colour; fine sheen on veneers but inclined to shrinkage.

Bubinga. W. Africa; pale to deep red, or purple with occasional light stripes; much used in 1930's, invariably in veneers; rotary cut bubinga is known as kavesingo.

Chestnut (Spanish, Sweet). Used as a substitute for oak and as core for veneers; practically free from warping.

Crabwood. British Guiana; reddish brown, straight-grained, works and polishes well; resembles mahogany.

Douglas Fir (Oregon Pine). N. W. America; reddish yellow to deep orange brown; attractive variable grain; light and strong, very suitable for panelling as free from warping and shrinkage.

Gaboon. Africa; golden brown to pinkish; good crotch figures.

Guarea. W. Africa; pinkish brown with white sapwood; attractive straight or wavy grain, fine texture like Cuban mahogany, but harder.

Gumwood. Southern States, U.S.A.; very hard; extensive use for veneer cores, crossbanding and carcase work.

Hemlock, Western. N. W. America; pale yellow, well marked growth rings; light and strong.

Idigbo (Black Afara, Emeri, Framire). W. Africa; pale yellow, occasional brown stripes; like plain sawn oak; similar to afara but harder and heavier.

Imbuya (Brazilian Walnut). S. America; olive to chocolate brown; not true walnut.

Indian Laurel. India and Burma; dark brown, bleaching to light brown with darker wavy streaks; richly figured veneers.

Iroko. E. and W. Africa; light yellowish to dark brown; stable and resistant to decay; about as strong as oak. Sometimes known as African teak or African oak.

Jarrah. S. W. Australia; reddish brown to dark mahogany; turns and carves well.

Mahogany, African. W. Africa; not true mahogany (i.e., Cuban, or 'Spanish', and Honduras), but most readily available of mahogany substitutes; light pink brown to deep red brown.

Makore (Cherry Mahogany). W. Africa; pale pinkish to dark purple brown with lustrous surface; resembles mahogany but heavier and harder.

Mansonia (Nigerian Walnut). W. Africa; dark grey brown, with light and dark bands; smooth texture and straight grained; closely resembles American black walnut and widely used as substitute for it.

Maple, Bird's Eye (American Sugar Maple). N. E. America; 'bird's eye' figure, caused by buds unable to force their way through the bark, are usually cut to veneer; favourite wood of late Victorian period.

Muninga (African Padouk). E. Africa; golden brown, with ripples of dark red brown; attractive wood, limited in supply; like padouk, but softer and lighter.

Oak, Japanese. Yellowish brown; lighter and milder than English oak but more easily worked, and widely used.

Oak, Slavonian (formerly called Austrian Oak). C. Europe; fine figure and easy to work; softer and lighter in colour than English oak; considered best type of oak for furniture today.

Obeche. W. Africa; white to pale yellow; soft and easily worked; veneers and plywood cores; stains well to imitate mahogany, as it has similar grain.

Padouk. Burma, Africa, Andaman Islands; see also Muninga. African variety has reddest colour; Burma variety is heavier, harder and lighter in colour than others.

Sapele (Sapele Mahogany). Tropical Africa; dark reddish brown, with regular narrow striped figure; excellent polish, and much used for cabinet work.

Silky Oak. Australia; light brown, silvery flecks, high lustre; superficially like English oak, but no botanical relationship.

Teak. Burma, Siam, India, Indo-China, Java; well-known for its outstanding durability; favourite wood in recent years for Danish machine-produced furniture.

Utile. W. Africa; dark reddish brown, closely resembling sapele, but with less regular grain and figure.

THE
BOOK OF
ENGLISH CHINA

Contents

List of Plates

A group of pottery and porcelain

PORCELAIN

Sources of the pieces illustrated are as follows:
Museum of the Royal Institution of Cornwall, Truro: Figs. 2, 3, 17, 18, 22, 23, 25, 26, 33, 34, 36, 38, 41, 42, 43, 44, 45, 47, 49, 50, 55, 60, 64, 70, 71, 72, 79, 80, 82, 84, 85, 86, 87, 88, 90, 93, 94, 95, 96, 97, 101, 105, 106, 107, 119, 122, 123, 125, 128, 132.
City Museum and Art Gallery, Plymouth: Figs. 4, 10, 20, 24, 39, 46, 51, 57, 65, 69, 73, 74, 75, 81, 83, 91, 99, 111, 114, 115, 116, 117, 124, 126, 131.
Victoria and Albert Museum, London: Figs. 1, 5, 6, 40, 52, 53, 76, 129, 130.
The National Trust (Fenton House, Hampstead): Figs. 54, 67, 118.
Josiah Wedgwood & Sons, Ltd, Barlaston, Staffs.: Figs. 31, 35, 37.
Royal Albert Memorial Museum, Exeter: Fig. 7.
Author: Frontispiece; Figs. 8, 9, 11, 12, 13, 14, 15, 16, 19, 21, 27, 28, 29, 30, 32, 48, 56, 58, 59, 61, 62, 63, 66, 68, 77, 78, 89, 92, 98, 100, 102, 103, 104, 108, 109, 110, 112, 113, 120, 121, 127.

Introduction

In this book the word China is deliberately used to describe both Pottery and Porcelain. In simple terms, the difference is that pottery is baked clay, and true porcelain is composed of a baked mixture of particular kinds of ground-up stone and clay (china-stone and china-clay) which combine when heated to a sufficiently high temperature. Alternatively, a type of porcelain, sometimes called 'soft paste' or artificial porcelain, can be made from glass and clay. In England, all except that made at Plymouth and Bristol (pages 86 to 92) was of the 'soft' variety, and the West Country factory founded by William Cookworthy stands alone for having made true porcelain.

The pieces illustrated have been selected to show a range of the different types of china made in England between about 1500 and 1830. In any anthology, whether of the written word or of pictures of objects of art, much has to be omitted for want of space and it is impossible to please every reader or even for the compiler to satisfy himself. In this instance the photographs are reproduced on a large scale, but not larger than their actual size. This makes them of more value, but of course reduces their number and adds to the difficulty of selection. The introductory notes to each section have been kept brief and so have the captions, but each of the latter includes the size of the piece shown and the approximate date of its manufacture.

The presence of marks is noted, but it should be observed that features such as the bases of figures and groups as well as the handles of teapots, sauceboats, cups and tankards are frequently of individual design used by one particular factory or maker. For identifying the origin of specimens these distinctive points can be more helpful than marks which, more often than not, are disappointingly absent.

Acknowledgments

Over one hundred of the photographs have been taken specially for this book, and thanks are due to the following for allowing the photographing of specimens in their care and for assisting in handling them: Mr H. L. Douch, Curator of the Museum of the Royal Institution of Cornwall, Truro; Mr A. A. Cumming, Curator of the City Museum and Art Gallery, Plymouth; and Dr R. C. Blackie, Curator of the Royal Albert Memorial Museum, Exeter. It is appropriate that the majority of the illustrations show pieces from collections in the West Country, whence came supplies of the clay and stone that form the substance of many of the wares.

For use of the remaining photographs thanks are due to: The Director of the Victoria and Albert Museum, London; The National Trust (pieces at Fenton House, Hampstead); Josiah Wedgwood & Sons, Ltd, Barlaston; and for allowing reproduction of illustrations that have appeared in the pages of their journals: Mr L. G. G. Ramsey, F.S.A., Editor of *The Connoisseur*, and Mr Denys Sutton, Editor of *Apollo*.

Factories and Dates

POTTERY

Factories, large and small, were so numerous that it is not possible to give their dates individually. The following is a list of the principal types of ware and the approximate dates during which they were made:

'PEASANT' WARE (lead-glazed): from medieval times to the present day, but the main interest for the collector lies in pieces made during the seventeenth and in the first part of the eighteenth centuries.

DELFTWARE (tin-glazed): from about 1600 until the end of the eighteenth century.

CREAMWARE: from about 1750 this was developed in Staffordshire, and by 1765 Josiah Wedgwood had evolved from it his famous Queen's Ware. It remained popular until gradually ousted by a white-bodied pottery from about 1800.

STONEWARE (salt-glazed): from the last quarter of the seventeenth century for about a hundred years, but it continued to be made for domestic and commercial uses. It is manufactured to-day for such things as drain-pipes, and until recently was used widely for 'stone' ginger-beer bottles. Wedgwood's superior type of stoneware, which he named Jasperware, was introduced about 1775 and is still made by the firm he founded.

PORCELAIN

CHELSEA	1745 to 1784	1745 to 1749	Triangle mark
		1749 to 1752	Raised anchor
		1753 to 1757	Red anchor
		1758 to 1769	Gold anchor
		1770 to 1784	Chelsea-Derby
'GIRL IN A SWING'	1749 to 1754		
BOW	after 1745 to 1775 or 1776		
DERBY	1750 to 1848	1784 to 1811 crowned 'D' and batons mark: the 'Crown Derby' period	
LUND'S BRISTOL	1749 to 1752		
WORCESTER	1751 to the present day	1751 to 1783 'Dr Wall' period 1783 onwards (see page 66)	
LONGTON HALL	1749 to 1760		
LIVERPOOL	about 1756 to 1840		
LOWESTOFT	1757 to 1802		
CAUGHLEY	1772 to 1814		
PLYMOUTH	1768 to 1770		
BRISTOL	1770 to 1781		
NEW HALL	1781 until about 1835		
COALPORT	about 1797		
MINTONS	about 1798 to the present day		
SPODE	about 1800, bought in 1833 by W. T. Copeland and continued under that name		
NANTGARW AND SWANSEA	1813 to 1822		
ROCKINGHAM	about 1820 to 1842		

1. Middle Bronze Age burial urn decorated by pressing cord on to the damp clay before firing. Excavated at Bere Regis, Dorset. 10½ inches high.

Pottery

MEDIEVAL TO TUDOR

A surprisingly large quantity of pottery dating back some hundreds of years has survived the passage of time, and most museums in London and elsewhere exhibit specimens from their immediate vicinity and farther afield. It will be seen that both shaping and decoration are simple, the use of a coating of glaze not only enhancing the appearance of an article, but proving essential if it were to be watertight.

The glaze contained some oxide of lead as an ingredient and for that reason pieces covered in it, which continued to be manufactured commercially into the nineteenth century, are described sometimes as 'lead-glazed'. Additions of certain substances (manganese, copper, etc.) produced coloured glazes. A completely glass-like and colourless glaze was not obtainable because of the presence of impurities which defied removal, and an amber tint was the nearest to it that was achieved.

Sometimes designs were cut into the soft clay, before it was put in the kiln for baking and hardening, by impressing it with a piece of cord (Fig. 1), or with an instrument. At a later date, a flat surface, such as that of a tile, could be moulded with a pattern cut in wood or stone (Fig. 3).

2. Tall jug covered in a green glaze on the outside and with a clear glaze inside, the edge of the base impressed with a pattern of finger-prints. Early sixteenth century. Excavated at Nottingham. 11 inches high.

3. Yellow-glazed tile with a raised design showing the Tudor Rose beneath a crown flanked by the initials of Queen Elizabeth I, with her coat-of-arms and supporters. Late sixteenth century. 13½ by 10 inches.

'PEASANT' WARE

These red and white clay pieces were the immediate successors to the preceding, and ample supplies of clay and fuel led to their manufacture concentrating eventually in Staffordshire. Whereas earlier pottery had been fired with wood, of which enormous quantities were needed for the purpose, this became scarce and from about the middle of the seventeenth century coal was used increasingly. The noticeably simple modelling and decoration has led to this type of pottery being labelled conveniently 'peasant' ware. Various types of ornament were popular, especially those using 'slip'—clay in liquid form which could be applied to a piece like sugar-icing to a cake (Figs 4, 5 and 6).

4. Staffordshire red clay dish with cream-coloured slip decoration, inscribed
RALPH SIMSON. About 1700. 17 inches diameter.

Slip of a contrasting colour was used also to cover an article completely and was then scratched through to show the design in the colour of the under-surface. This technique is called 'sgraffito', from the Italian, and potteries in the West of England, at Barnstaple and elsewhere, specialised in making such pieces until quite recent times (Fig. 7).

Some of the Staffordshire potters inscribed the names of their friends or of themselves on their work, and those of the Toft, Shaw and Simpson families (often mis-spelled as in Fig. 4), and others have been noted. In Kent, Wrotham was another important potting centre, many pieces from there bearing initials and dates between about 1600 and 1750 (Fig. 6).

Many of the surviving specimens of 'peasant' ware are elaborate in both shape and ornament, and their decorative quality has ensured their careful treatment. Most of them were made as gifts for special occasions, usually local ones: young potters presented them to their sweethearts; and weddings, christenings (Fig. 5), and other family events were celebrated. They were sometimes treasured as heirlooms long after whatever occasioned their making had been forgotten, and half a century or so ago examples were to be found in the cottages of Staffordshire and elsewhere in the vicinity of old potteries. The rougher wares made for everyday use, simple in design and plain in appearance, have nearly all disappeared.

5. Staffordshire cream-coloured clay cradle with red slip decoration, made as a christening gift. About 1700. 10¾ inches long.

6. Wrotham (Kent) red and cream clay three-handled cup, known as a 'Tyg', dated 1621. 6⅝ inches high.

7. West Country red and cream-coloured clay Harvest jug with sgraffito decoration. 14 inches high. Under the handle it is inscribed:

> 'Harvis is cam all bissey
> Now in mackin of your
> Barly mow when men do
> Laber hard and swet good
> Ale is better far than meet
> Bideford   April 28
> 1775   M—W.'

DELFTWARE

This type of pottery takes its name from the Dutch town, the centre of the potting industry in Holland, where the Italian method of coating pieces with a glaze rendered opaque by the use of an oxide of tin was practised. The glaze on top of ordinary clay gave a white surface which could be painted in a range of colours, and was a great advance over the transparent lead glazes otherwise employed. Pieces decorated in this manner are referred to sometimes as 'tin-glazed' or as 'delftware'; the latter with a small 'd' to distinguish them from Dutch-made Delftware.

8. Charger decorated in colours showing Adam and Eve and the Serpent. About 1650. 15¾ inches diameter.

The process was used in England by 1600 and during the whole of the seventeenth and eighteenth centuries. Important centres of manufacture were in London, notably at Lambeth, where there were a number of potteries, and at Liverpool, Bristol, Wincanton (Somerset) and Dublin. It is thought, not unreasonably, that specimens painted with the coats-of-arms of City Companies were made in London (Figs 10 and 11).

Tin-glazed pottery is recognised easily by the fact that raw edges, underneath plates and jugs for instance, reveal the rough clay forming the body of the article. The fact that the glaze is liable to chip away in use is seen in a large proportion of surviving pieces which have damaged rims (Figs 13 and 16 for instance). This unfortunate weakness led to its replacement by the less-vulnerable cream-ware and by porcelain.

While some delftware was decorated in attractive bright red, green, yellow, brown and blue, much was painted in blue alone in imitation of imported Chinese porcelain, which was copied not only in colour, but also in shape and in the range of subjects depicted. Most of the output was of pieces for use at the table, and plates survive in large numbers. Big dishes, known as chargers and made more for decoration than for use (Fig. 8), were produced throughout the seventeenth century, and punch-bowls (Fig. 13) were popular from after about 1700.

9. Dish commemorating the coronation of King William III and Queen Mary, painted in blue, with 'portraits' and initials. About 1689. 8½ inches diameter.

10. Slab for grinding pills, painted in blue, with the arms of the Apothecaries' Society of London. The motto may be translated: 'Throughout the world I am called the bringer of aid'. Late seventeenth century. $10\frac{1}{4}$ inches high.

11. Tankard, painted in blue, with the arms of the Blacksmiths' Company of London. Inscribed: 'Brother Vilckin Let Us Drink Whilst Wee Have Breath For There's No Drinking AFter Death: Joseph Piper: 1752'. 7¼ inches high.

Examples of eighteenth century china, all in the author's collection.

12. Bristol plate, painted in colours, with a seated Chinese figure. About 1750. 9 inches diameter.

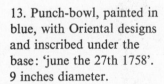

13. Punch-bowl, painted in blue, with Oriental designs and inscribed under the base: 'june the 27th 1758'. 9 inches diameter.

14. Vase with 'mimosa' pattern painted in blue. About 1750. 7 inches high.

15. Liverpool wall-tile printed in black. Late eighteenth century. 4¾ inches square.

16. Eighteenth-century ointment pot, dug out of a garden in 1962. 2 inches diameter.

STONEWARE

Stoneware was imported into England from Germany from the sixteenth century, and took the form of jugs and drinking-vessels. They are of a whitish-grey colour, their composition being clay fired to a very high temperature and glazed, when considered necessary, by the simple method of throwing a quantity of common salt into the kiln while the ware was baking. The resulting product, known as 'salt-glazed stoneware', is a distinctive material with a thin glaze that does not obscure any pattern on it, and that often has a finely-pitted surface comparable with that of orange peel (Fig. 19).

John Dwight of Fulham was granted a patent for making an English imitation of the German product in 1671, and a few pieces undoubtedly of his manufacture have survived. His pottery was carried on by successive owners, and among their specialities were tankards with raised ornaments further decorated with washes of brown-tinted clay (Fig. 19). Brown-coloured wares were made also in Nottingham from about 1700 (Fig. 18) and in other places.

In Staffordshire, improvements were made in stoneware in order to compete with porcelain, and a whiter variety was evolved by about 1730. Unusual and attractive designs were produced and colouring was attempted with success. This was either in a full range with a rich pink and a turquoise-blue predominating, or in what is termed 'scratch blue'—a pattern being scratched in the clay and dusted with powdered blue pigment (Fig. 22). Another variety of stoneware is dark red in colour; it originated in China where teapots of the material were made and exported with consignments of tea. The idea that the beverage tasted better and was more beneficial when brewed in a redware pot came into favour, and Dwight as well as two Dutch brothers who came to England, John and David Elers, were prominent in making a pottery of this type (Fig. 17). It was made also in Germany and Holland, and it is difficult to be certain in some instances where the surviving pieces originated.

17. Unglazed red stoneware mug with raised decoration of a sprig of blossom. About 1700. 3½ inches high.

18. Nottingham brown-glazed mug with pierced ornament. About 1700. 4⅛ inches high.

19. Fulham tankard coloured in shades of brown and decorated with a bust of
Queen Anne and a huntsman with hounds and a stag. Inscribed round the top:
'Drink to the Pious Memory of Good Queen Ann, July y^e 25: 1729' (Queen
Anne died in 1714). 8$\frac{1}{4}$ inches high.

20. Jug with a coloured design of flowers, initials and the curious wording:
'One Iugg more and then 1766'. 7¾ inches high.

21. Cup and cover in the form of a bear seated hugging a dog, the fur of the animals imitated with shreds of clay. About 1740. 3¼ inches high.

22. Hollow 'brick' with a pierced top and 'scratch-blue' decoration. Filled with sand, it would have served as a stand for quill pens, and filled with water for flowers. About 1750. 6¾ inches long.

23. Sauceboat moulded with a pattern of scrolls on a chequered ground, the former coloured. About 1750.
8½ inches long.

24. Teapot painted in white on a dark blue ground. About 1750. 6¾ inches long.

CREAMWARE

The search for better products with which to meet the increasing competition of porcelain led to the introduction about the middle of the eighteenth century of a ware with a cream-coloured body. This was developed from the white clay, often used in the form of 'slip' and familiar to the makers of 'peasant' pieces for a century or more (Figs 4, 5, 6 and 7); the name of Thomas Astbury is associated with the improvement. This creamware was covered in transparent coloured lead glazes which were usually dabbed on to give a blotched effect that is far more pleasing than it sounds.

The foremost potter in the evolution of this ware and its glazes was Thomas Whieldon, but he did not mark his productions and positive identification is seldom possible. He was followed by two men, father and son, both named Ralph Wood, whose figures and groups have achieved for them a lasting fame (Figs 28 and 30). This is not only because of the originality of the models, but because they were the first to control the colours carefully and give them a more natural effect (compare Fig. 26 with 28). A small proportion of the Woods' pieces are marked with a stamp bearing their names, and others have a tiny raised representation of a group of trees—a punning play on their surname.

26. A Turk, streaked with brown and green glazes. About 1750. 5¾ inches high.

25. Figure of a seated cat with brown and olive-green markings. About 1750. 4 inches high.

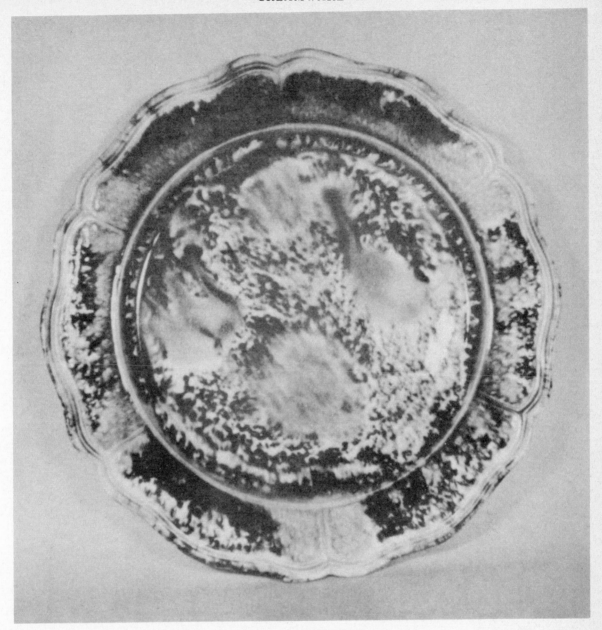

27. Plate decorated with glazes of brown, green and grey to give the effect of tortoiseshell. About 1760. 9¾ inches diameter.

28. A flute-player with a shepherdess and animals, made by Ralph Wood and
decorated with coloured glazes. About 1775. $9\frac{3}{4}$ inches high.

29. The familiar Toby-jug was modelled first from an engraving of a character named Toby Philpot commemmorated in some verses published in 1761. There are many different versions of the jug; this one is called 'The Sailor' About 1780. 11½ inches high.

30. Group of a terrier baiting a bull; at the back is stamped 'Ra. Wood'. About 1775. 5¾ inches high. This group is typical of the work of the Woods; the pale-coloured washes of glaze with a brilliant sheen accentuating the neat potting. Other homely subjects, sporting and otherwise, were modelled, and the makers appealed to a more cultured market with figures of gods and goddesses decorated in a similar manner.

WEDGWOOD

Josiah Wedgwood merits a section to himself in any consideration of eighteenth-century English pottery. He spread the fame of Staffordshire throughout the world, and by his skill, industry and inventiveness both his own name and the firm he founded have endured to the present day. He was in partnership with Thomas Whieldon for a few years, but by 1759 had started his own pottery where he made wares of types similar to those of his neighbours and competitors. Although unmarked, Wedgwood's are recognised by their superior potting and the greater brilliance of their glazes (Figs 33 and 34).

In 1765, a cream-coloured ware, which he evolved from the creamwares of Whieldon and the Woods (pages 30 to 34), was named 'Queen's Ware' after Queen Charlotte had purchased some pieces of it. In a short time this became immensely popular and, whether entirely plain or with sparse but tasteful decoration, was to be found in homes in every known land.

31. Josiah Wedgwood, 1730–1795, modelled when he was 47 years old.

As the result of a friendship with a Liverpool man, Thomas Bentley, who had a keen appreciation of the Antique with which Wedgwood became inspired, the two men formed a partnership. A new factory named Etruria was built at Burslem in 1769, and here were made the special types of stoneware with which the name of Wedgwood is linked: basaltes named after the black stone it resembles, and the series of coloured jasperwares used to make the well-known vases, plaques and other pieces ornamented with reliefs. The most famous of these are undoubtedly the copies of the Portland Vase, of which the original is in the British Museum, begun in 1786 and not finished until four years later (Fig. 37). Fewer than twenty of the first series of copies have been located, but large numbers of less carefully made ones have been turned out subsequently. Until Bentley's death in 1780 the names of both men were stamped on their Etruria productions, but creamware has that of Wedgwood alone and so have jasperwares and basaltes made after 1780.

The firm of Wedgwood still makes many thousands of pieces each year in the old patterns, as it has done continuously since the time of Josiah, and it is not always easy for the inexperienced to tell old from new, or from copies made in the nineteenth century. It is helpful to know that since about 1760 the majority of pieces have been marked, and this makes it easy to distinguish the work of the many copyists (Fig. 39). One point is worth remembering—specimens stamped with the word ENGLAND as well as WEDGWOOD were made after 1891, when an American law required imports to bear the name of the country of origin.

32. Jasperware buttons. About 1780. Approximately ⅝ inch high. Like most of Wedgwood's productions these were made for use; among the items manufactured in jasperware were small pieces such as beads, seals and scent-bottles, as well as plaques for mounting, in polished steel or precious metals, as brooches, buckles and watch-cases.

33. Teapot in the form of a pineapple, covered in green and yellow glazes. About 1760.
4½ inches high.

34. Teapot in the form of a cauliflower, covered partly in a green glaze. About
1760. 4½ inches high.

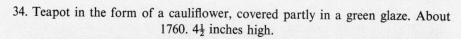

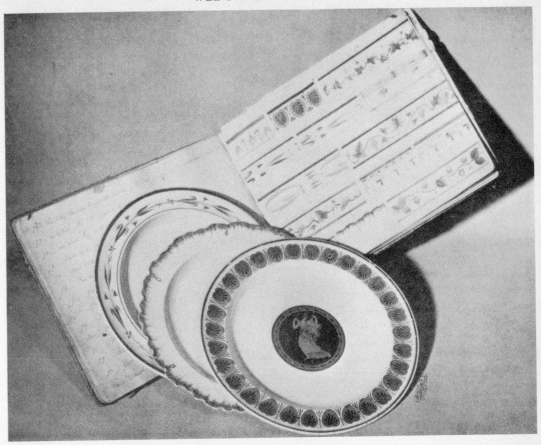

35. A group of decorated Queen's Ware plates, marked **WEDGWOOD**, with Josiah Wedgwood's original pattern-book of 1770. Plates, 10 inches diameter.

36. Blue and white jasperware butter-dish, cover and stand, marked WEDGWOOD. About 1785. Stand, $6\frac{7}{8}$ inches diameter.

37. The Portland Vase. The original, which is made of dark blue and white Roman glass, has been reproduced many times since the late eighteenth century. This was Josiah Wedgwood's own copy, made under his supervision in 1790. 10 inches high.

38. Red (*Rosso antico*) and
black (*Basaltes*) stoneware milk
jug, marked WEDGWOOD.
About 1820. 5¾ inches long.

39. Black stoneware tea-kettle,
unmarked. Made by one of
Wedgwood's many
imitators, perhaps Humphrey
Palmer of Hanley. About 1790.
7¼ inches high.

LEEDS

The pottery at Leeds in Yorkshire made a creamware similar in appearance to that popularised by Josiah Wedgwood. Decoration often took the form of moulded scrolled borders and carefully finished pierced patterns (Fig. 40). Much of the output was left uncoloured, but painted pieces are often in a combination of brownish-red and black (Fig. 41).

Some of the ware is indistinguishable from that made by potters in Staffordshire, Liverpool and elsewhere, but a small proportion bears the mark LEEDS POTTERY, which is found sometimes stamped twice in the form of a cross. The factory continued in production until 1878 and made copies of its earlier pieces which have deceived many collectors.

40. Creamware butter-dish with cover and stand, the knob appropriately in the form of a cow and the cover decorated with a pierced pattern. About 1790. Stand, 7¼ inches long.

41. Creamware teapot with coloured decoration. About 1780. 5 inches high.

EARLY NINETEENTH CENTURY

The early years of the nineteenth century saw new factories opening and old ones continuing to develop. The greatest improvement was the making of a white-bodied glazed earthenware which was decorated, usually in blue, by means of printed patterns (see page 65). It was well made, but intended to be sold cheaply, and the firms of Spode and Wedgwood competed with dozens of others in Staffordshire and elsewhere to supply eager buyers on both sides of the Atlantic. Almost as popular were the Stone-china of Spode and Mason's Ironstone China, both of which were very durable; the latter was usually decorated floridly with Oriental designs in red and vivid blue.

More for decoration than utility were pieces covered in lustre glazes—copper (Figs 43 and 44) and silver—which continue to be made to the present day. Mantelpiece ornaments differed little in design from those of earlier date, but their colours were more garish, with the pale washes of lead glaze supplanted by realistic painting in harsher shades applied on top of a clear glaze (Figs 45 and 46). A few factories continued to make wares of a higher quality than the average, and among these Swansea is noteworthy (Fig. 42).

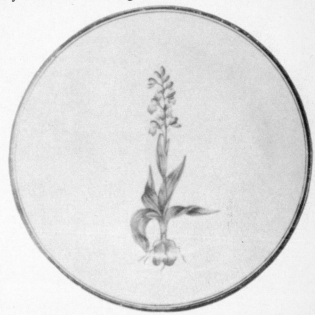

42. Swansea plate painted in colours, the name of the plant 'Dwarf Orchis' written in red on the back. About 1800. 7¾ inches diameter.

43. Staffordshire goblet decorated in copper lustre. About 1830. 5 inches high.

44. Staffordshire jug moulded with figures of sportsmen with a dog, and painted in colours and lustre. About 1820. 5½ inches high.

45. Staffordshire figure of a youth painted in colours over the glaze. About 1800.
8½ inches high.

46. Staffordshire figure of a seated lion. About 1825. 4¼ inches high.

47. Bristol puzzle-jug with coloured decoration. About 1820. 5 inches high.

48. Plate printed in blue with an imaginary landscape, impressed mark: SPODE. About 1810. 10 inches diameter.

Porcelain

CHELSEA

The factory was in existence by 1745; a few cream jugs have survived which are incised beneath the base with that date, a triangle and the word 'Chelsea'. Other pieces marked with a triangle alone are known, and all share a pleasant milk-white appearance and a shining glaze.

By 1749 announcements in newspapers linked the name of a Belgian-born silversmith, Nicholas Sprimont, with the factory. He was manager for a few years, and after 1758 became proprietor. From 1749 pieces were marked with a small anchor moulded on a raised oval pad (can this choice of emblem be attributed to the Thames-side situation of the works?), but soon the raised anchor was outlined in red (Fig. 52). Then, from 1753 to 1757, it was painted direct in red on a flat part of the object, and often is so insignificant as to be overlooked.

Pieces with the triangle or raised anchor are rare, and both marks are found mostly on useful articles such as salt-cellars, cups and saucers and teapots. A few figures were made, and like the other pieces were sometimes left unpainted. The red anchor period saw the finest of Chelsea porcelain, and the figures and groups have been described with reason as being among the best made in all Europe. While many were copied from Dresden originals (Fig. 53), others were completely new, and the creation of some of them has been discovered recently to have been the work of another Belgian-born craftsman, a man named Joseph Willems who was known here by his anglicised surname of Williams.

The final period, which began in about 1758, was notable for the use of lavish decoration both in painting and gilding. The mark was an anchor in gold, and productions included elaborately designed vases as well as figures and groups.

Mention must be made of the famous miniature pieces often known now by their eighteenth-century name of 'Toys'—a word that did not then mean only children's playthings, but trifles. They included not only seals and scent-bottles, but snuff-boxes, needle-cases, pipe-stoppers and similar small-sized articles that are usually more decorative than useful, but are nonetheless delightful.

Sprimont sold the factory in 1769, and eventually it was bought by William Duesbury of Derby, who carried it on until 1784. During his ownership a mark in the form of a capital 'D' combined with an anchor was used.

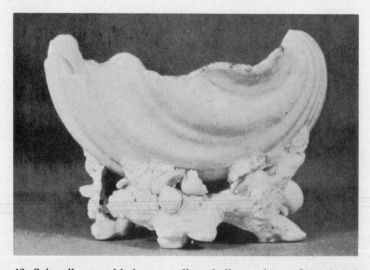

49. Salt-cellar moulded as a scallop shell on a base of coral and
sea-shells. About 1750. 3¼ inches long.

50. Cream jug modelled with two seated goats and with a bee, known as a 'Goat and Bee' jug, marked with a triangle incised under the base. About 1745. 4¼ inches high.

51. Box and cover in the form of an apple with a caterpillar for the handle, marked inside the lid with a small anchor in red. About 1755. 4 inches high.

52. Figure of a warbler, marked with a raised anchor outlined in red (visible to the right of the base). About 1750. 5¼ inches high.

53. Group of a woman dancing with a masked man, copied from a Dresden original of about 1740 and marked with an anchor in red. About 1755. 7 inches high.

54. Figures of a shepherd and a shepherdess, marked with an anchor in gold. About 1760. 11 and 11½ inches high.

55. Plate painted in the centre with an exotic bird, the border with coloured flowers and with insects in gold on panels of deep blue, marked with an anchor in gold. Of similar design to plates in a service given by George III and Queen Charlotte to the brother of the latter, the Duke of Mecklenburg-Strelitz, in 1763. $8\frac{3}{4}$ inches diameter.

56. A group of 'Toys': (Left to right) Snuff-box modelled with a boy playing a flute with sheep beside him; scent-bottle designed as fish in a net; three seals, that on the right representing the Marquis of Granby. All about 1760. Box, $2\frac{3}{4}$ inches long; bottle, $3\frac{3}{4}$ inches high; seals, $1\frac{1}{4}$ inches high.

'GIRL IN A SWING' FACTORY

A number of figures and groups with details in common have been assumed to be the productions of a rival factory to Sprimont's, situated also in Chelsea, working between about 1749 and 1754. A noted example is a figure of a girl seated on a swing between two trees, and the whole series of pieces, of which fewer than one hundred have so far come to light, is known as the 'girl in a swing' type (Fig. 57).

It has been shown recently that this 'second Chelsea' factory made 'Toys', and it has been suggested that the idea of making miniature pieces in England originated at the rival factory and was copied later by Sprimont.

57. Group of Europa and the Bull of 'Girl in a Swing' type. About 1750. $6\frac{1}{2}$ inches high.

BOW

The starting of the factory at Stratford-le-Bow, in the east of London, was the result of patents taken out in 1744 and 1749 by Thomas Frye (Fig. 58). He was a versatile Irishman, who painted portraits and miniatures and made engravings, and became manager of the factory when it opened sometime after 1745 until he retired in 1759.

Much of the output was of pieces decorated in blue for everyday use at the table. Figures and groups included many copying those imported from Dresden and others of distinctively original design, among them some that were quite as decorative as any made elsewhere. On the whole, however, the porcelain made at Bow is less sophisticated in appearance and only rarely as well finished as that of its rival, Chelsea, but it has an undeniable honest charm that has earned it popularity for two hundred years.

As was the case with other factories, many of the earliest examples were left white and uncoloured, but later ones were usually painted. An opaque middle shade of blue was very popular when contrasted with lemon-yellow, the bases of groups and figures were often lined in a purplish-red, and gilding was applied sparingly in most instances. There was no regular factory mark, but figures sometimes have an anchor and a dagger painted in red, or a blue crescent under the base; the latter is sometimes confused with the similar Worcester crescent, but figures from the latter factory were never marked. Many Bow figures have a square hole at the back for the insertion of a metal candle-holder.

The factory closed in either 1775 or 1776.

58. Engraved self-portrait of Thomas Frye, 1710–1762.

THE BOW CHINA WAREHOUSE was opened on Wednesday last, near the Royal Exchange, in Cornhill, with a back Door facing the Bank in Threadneedle-Street, for the Convenience of all Customers, both in Town and Country, where it will continue to be sold in the same Manner as formerly at Bow, with Allowance made to wholesale Dealers.

59. From a newspaper of February, 1753.

60. An actress in Turkish costume. About 1750. 8½ inches high.

61. Plate with a design copied from Chinese porcelain painted in blue. About 1750. 9 inches diameter.

62. Tankard, painted in blue, with
an English version of an
Oriental scene. About 1755.
5 inches high.

63. Sauceboat moulded with
flowers and decorated with
gilding. About 1755.
$8\frac{3}{4}$ inches long.

64. Group of a woman and a child bearing sheaves of corn, symbolical of
Summer. About 1760. 7½ inches high.

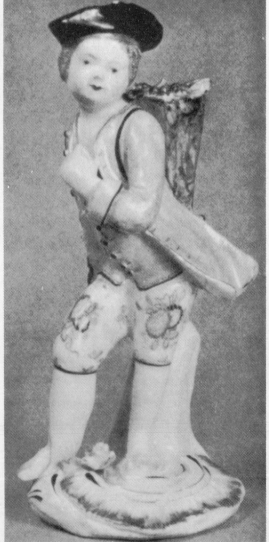

65. Candlestick modelled with a kneeling figure of Cupid reaching up to a bird nesting in a bush. About 1765. 9¾ inches high.

66. Figure of a boy carrying a pannier of grapes, perhaps symbolising Autumn. About 1760. 6¼ inches high.

67. A gardener and his companion, symbolising Autumn and Spring. About 1770. 12½ and 13 inches high.

DERBY

As at Chelsea, cream jugs are the first wares that can be regarded with certainty as having been made at Derby. A few have survived which bear the word 'Derby' or an initial 'D' and the date 1750 on them, and some figures and groups have been identified also as productions of the years between 1750 and 1756. These latter pieces are unmarked, but have some features in common with one another, including a peculiarly dry outer edge at the base and, unless left white, were decorated in pale colours.

In 1756 the factory came into the ownership of William Duesbury, who had worked for some years in London decorating porcelain bought from various sources. Under his direction Derby became noted for figures and groups which were advertised in newspapers of the time as 'the second Dresden'.

The white unglazed ware known as 'biscuit' was introduced about 1770 (Fig. 74). As there was neither glaze nor colouring to conceal roughness or defects each specimen had to be finished with especial care and, in consequence, was sold at a higher price than a comparable coloured one. Derby grew celebrated also for the ornamental vases, services and cabinet cups and saucers that were painted with minute care in a variety of patterns. These and the later groups and figures show many signs of the Classical taste that became fashionable from about 1770. Honeysuckle blossom and other Grecian *motifs* appeared in the borders of plates, and bases composed of scrolls and shells were replaced by those of severely plain type (Figs 74 and 75).

Following his death in 1786 Duesbury was succeeded by his son, also named William, and in 1811 the factory was sold to its manager, Robert Bloor. The quality of its products then began to decline and the concern closed in 1848.

While the earliest figures have the 'dry edge' noted above, later ones invariably show under the base three round marks where they stood on pads in the kiln. Their colouring is lively, and frequently includes a turquoise blue that tends to flake off or turn brown with age. After about 1770 figures were marked with a pattern number incised under the base, and from the time when the Chelsea factory was bought by Duesbury, the mark of a 'D' combined with an anchor was used. Following the closing of the London works in 1784, a mark showing a pair of crossed batons, some dots and a crowned 'D' was painted in red or blue. It was in use until 1811 and gave its name to the so-called 'Crown Derby' period.

AT WILLIAMS's Cool Retreat, formerly Oliver Cromwell's Palace, facing Craig's Cour, Charing-cross, being remarkably cooler than most Houses in London, There will be sold by Hand, a few Days longer, all the Remainder of his large Collection of Foreign China, with several new Chinese Curiosities never before exposed to Sale; with great Variety of India Japan Dressing-Boxes in compleat and other Sets; Japan Dressing Glasses, and a large Quantity of new-fashion'd Fans; there is also the greatest Variety of the Derby Porcelain or second Dresden Figures, Baskets, Leaves, &c. and several curious Pieces for Deserts, all mark'd by the Proprietor's Orders at the lowest Prices, with good Allowance to Dealers; several of the said Goods will be sold under prime Cost, rather than risque the moving; for Conveniency of Gentlemen and Ladies Carriages, the Door will be open'd in Spring Gardens.

68. From a newspaper of 1757.

69. Figure of a street-seller. About 1755. 5 inches high. The man carries a basket holding bottles of absinthe, and he is one of a series of Paris street-sellers copied from some made at Meissen (Dresden) in 1753. The German porcelain factory exported much of its output, and the figures were doubtless made to be sold in France. This English example has the typical dry edge round the base and is decorated in the pale colours used at Derby before about 1760.

70. Figure of a canary perced on a base decorated with flowers. About 1760. 5¼ inches high.

71. A sauceboat with floral decoration in colours. About 1770. 7½ inches long.

72. Stand for sweetmeats or pickles. About 1760. 9 inches high.

73. A sportsman with his dog. About 1770. 10¾ inches high.

74. A figure, in the white unglazed ware called 'biscuit', of a gardener, symbolising the element Earth. About 1775. 6½ inches high.

75. Pair of figures of a ewe and a ram. About 1780. 2½ inches high.

76. Covered vase decorated with panels of subjects in grey on a gold-striped
ground, marked with a crowned 'D' in gold. One of a set of three. About
1780. 13⅛ inches high.

LUND'S BRISTOL AND WORCESTER

It was found, perhaps by William Cookworthy (page 86), that the use of Cornish soapstone as an ingredient made an excellent porcelain. A factory for exploiting this discovery was opened in Bristol in 1749 by a man named Benjamin Lund; a factory known until recently by the name of a former occupant, a glassmaker called Lowdin, but which is now referred to more correctly as Lund's. In 1752 the factory and its secrets were acquired by a newly-formed company in Worcester, and the Bristol venture came to an end. One of the partners in the Midlands enterprise was a local physician of some eminence, Dr John Wall, who is remembered for giving his name to the china made at the factory during his lifetime and for some years following his death in 1776.

The wares made during the short period at Bristol include a few surviving figures and sauceboats with the word BRISTOLL embossed on them, and a quantity of tableware (cups, jugs and so forth) particularly delicately painted in blue or in other colours. Decoration was sparse but attractive, and was mostly of Oriental subjects.

Much of the early Worcester output was painted in blue, but by 1757 a new process made it possible to produce decorated ware cheaply. It is uncertain who actually discovered that a design printed on a special thin paper with special ink might be transferred to a piece of china, but some Worcester jugs with a portrait of the king of Prussia bear the date 1757 (Fig. 83). Thereafter printed decoration took its place alongside hand-painting, which remained in use for the better types of ware. By 1760 printing in blue under the glaze was in use, and again Worcester led the field, although other factories were quick to copy the idea.

The Dr Wall period of Worcester, which lasted roughly from 1752 to 1783, was notable for the high quality of its productions both in potting and in decoration. Tablewares and vases were the main output, although some figures were made between 1769 and 1771 and are now extremely rare (Fig. 87). Painting often took the form of shaped panels of exotic birds, figures or landscapes on grounds of various colours: blue, red, yellow, green, etc., some of which were drawn in the form of small scales and others were used in thick, even washes (Figs 84, 85 and 86). Gilding was distinctive, thick and rather dull, and is the feature that usually reveals a fake.

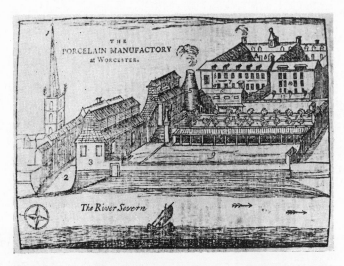

77. 'N.B. A sale of this manufacture will begin at the Worcester muſic meeting on Sept. 20, with great variety of ware, and, 'tis said, at a moderate price'.
From the *Gentleman's Magazine*, August, 1752.

78. The London
showroom of the
Worcester factory at
No. 1, Coventry
Street. A woodcut
illustration from a
book published in
1865.

In 1783 the factory was sold to its London agent, Thomas Flight, and during the ensuing years changed its style from time to time, as follows:

| 1783–1792 | Flight's | 1807–1813 | Barr, Flight & Barr |
| 1792–1807 | Flight & Barr | 1813–1840 | Flight, Barr & Barr |

Under these various owners the high quality of workmanship remained and the fashionable Classical style prevailed (Figs 124 and 128).

Soon after 1783 one of the painters, Humphrey Chamberlain, left the firm and founded one of his own, which in due course absorbed the original company and is in existence to-day.

Marks used in the Wall period included a fretted Chinese-looking square, an imitation of the Dresden crossed swords, the letter 'W', a crescent, and imitation Oriental characters, all in blue. Later pieces have either initials, such as F.B.B. for Flight, Barr & Barr, or a printed mark with name, address and other details in full. Chamberlain's ware was marked some-time with the name of the maker in red.

79. A small example of Lund's
Bristol sauceboat with moulded
and coloured decoration. About
1750. $4\frac{3}{8}$ inches long.

80. Lund's Bristol sauceboat with moulded and coloured decoration. About 1750. 7¾ inches long.

81. Lund's Bristol double-lipped sauceboat with moulded and coloured decoration, the handles topped with animals' heads. The shapes of this and Figs 79 and 80 are copied from silver originals. About 1750. 8¾ inches long.

82. Tankard with a Chinese landscape painted in a panel on a pale yellow ground. About 1765. $5\frac{3}{4}$ inches high.

83. Tankard with a portrait of Frederick the Great, King of Prussia, printed in black. Dated 1757. $4\frac{5}{8}$ inches high.

84. Cup and saucer with painted fruit and insects within a pea-green border. About 1775. Saucer, 5¼ inches diameter.

85. Cup and saucer with fruit and flowers painted within a claret-red and gilt border. About 1775. Saucer, 4¾ inches diameter.

86. Flower-holder with panels of flowers and an exotic bird painted on a scale-blue ground, marked with a fretted square in blue. About 1770. 6¾ inches high.

87. A sportswoman, one of the few figures made at Worcester between 1769 and 1771. It is unmarked, as are all the other known specimens. $7\frac{1}{4}$ inches high.

88. Plate with fruit and insects painted by an 'outside decorator': a man who bought china in the white from a factory and decorated it to his own taste or to the order of his clients. About 1775. 8¾ inches diameter.

89. Teapot, painted with a Japanese pattern, having a typical Worcester floral knob on the cover and marked with imitation Oriental characters in blue. About 1770. 6¼ inches high.

LONGTON HALL

This china works was started in 1749 and lasted for about ten years, but its existence was forgotten completely until some newspaper announcements of the 1750's were discovered and reprinted in 1881. A book on the subject of the factory, published in 1957, told of the dramatic finding of some of the original documents relating to its founding and the result of excavations on the actual site.

The porcelain has been called 'heavy and cold in tone' and the glaze compared with candle-wax, but specimens vary in appearance. They were not always very well finished; flaws that appeared in the kiln during preliminary firing were ignored by the painter and do not seem to have prevented purchase by eighteenth-century buyers. Some of the figures and many of the domestic pieces were of original design, and the latter sometimes took the form of overlapping leaves (Fig. 90), or embodied other vegetable forms.

A noticeably deep and strong blue was used, and this was overpainted occasionally with a thick white instead of the more usual gilding. Most pieces were left unmarked, but a small proportion bear two crossed 'L's' with three dots below in blue.

90. Sauceboat designed as a group of cabbage leaves with a twig handle. About 1755. 8½ inches long.

91. Tankard, painted in blue, with a Chinese figure holding a parasol. About 1755. 4 inches high.

92. Cup, painted in colours, with architecturally-improbable buildings of a kind often found on Longton Hall pieces. About 1755. 2½ inches high.

93. Pug-dog decorated under the glaze in blue and brown. About 1755. 3¾ inches high.

94. A girl dancing, her skirt painted in red stripes giving a vivid sense of movement. About 1755. 6¼ inches high.

95. Harlequin as a bagpiper. About 1755. 5¼ inches high.

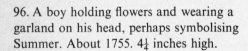

96. A boy holding flowers and wearing a garland on his head, perhaps symbolising Summer. About 1755. 4¼ inches high.

97. Hercules and the Lion, the separate (but original) stand painted with a Chinese scene. About 1755. 7¾ inches high over-all.

LIVERPOOL

In 1756 one of the principal workmen at Worcester was engaged to start a factory at Liverpool, and it can come as no surprise to learn that there is a strong resemblance between many of the wares from both places; both used Cornish soapstone as an ingredient. The porcelain from this factory, and from others in the city, is not of notably high quality; much was painted in blue and some in other colours, but without any great distinction of design or execution.

A large proportion of the output was exported to America and the West Indies, and doubtless was turned out in quantity to sell cheaply. None of the Liverpool factories used marks, and only in recent years has research decided what was made there, but problems still remain unsolved.

Liverpool was known also for the decoration of both pottery and porcelain with printed patterns, and from about 1760 a flourishing business was done in performing this service for Wedgwood and other makers (Fig. 15).

98. Sauceboat with blue printed decoration, the handle ending in a snake's head. About 1770. 7½ inches long.

99. Tall vase and cover with exotic birds painted in colours. About 1760. 15½ inches high. Such strange-looking birds were a popular subject with most factories. They were European versions of those on imported Oriental ware, which often had their origin in mythology rather than Nature.

100. Milk jug and a pair of pickle-trays or sweetmeat dishes decorated with flowers in blue. About 1770. Jug, 4¾ inches high.

101. Teapot with moulded and blue-painted decoration. About 1770. 7 inches high.

LOWESTOFT

This East Anglian factory was opened in 1757, and it is said that one of the partners was smuggled into the Bow works so that he could learn their secrets. Certainly, the two wares bear a strong resemblance to one another; not only are they alike in the porcelain itself, but both favoured painting in blue.

The Lowestoft factory has acquired a greater fame than its productions merit from having had its name given to a type of Chinese eighteenth-century porcelain made for export to the West. The story of its alleged English origin was told in a book published a hundred years ago, and although soon discredited the name 'Lowestoft' continues often to be applied to this Oriental ware.

True English Lowestoft was confined principally to domestic pieces, and although a few figures were made they cannot be claimed to have much interest. A proportion of the output was painted with names or initials and dates, many referring to local persons, which gives it a wider appeal than would otherwise be the case (Figs 102 and 106).

102 and 103. Inkwell with a spray of flowers, painted in blue, and *below* the inscribed base. 2⅞ inches diameter.

104. Saucer with a
dragon painted in blue.
About 1775. $5\frac{1}{8}$
inches diameter.

105. Milk jug with an Oriental
pattern painted in various colours.
About 1775. 3 inches high.

106. Teapot painted in colours and inscribed: 'Maria Hoyle NORWICH 1774'. 6½ inches high.

107. Cup and saucer painted with flowers in pink within a gilt border. Part of a teaset made for Robert Browne, one of the partners in the factory, for his wedding-day. About 1775. Saucer, 5 inches diameter.

CAUGHLEY

Thomas Turner, who had been employed at Worcester, began to make porcelain at Caughley (pronounced 'Coffley'), near Broseley, Shropshire, in about 1772. Early wares are like those of Worcester, but if held to the light Caughley is yellow or brown in tone, in contrast to the green tone of Worcester. Much was decorated in blue, either by hand-painting or printing, and among popular designs used there was numbered the well-known 'Willow Pattern', supposed to have been engraved first by Turner's pupil, Thomas Minton. No figures were made.

Marks used were a capital 'C' (for Caughley), which is mistaken sometimes for the Worcester crescent, an 'S' (for Salopian or Shropshire), and SALOPIAN impressed.

108. Dish with a pierced border and twig handles, and with printed and painted patterns in blue. Marked with a capital 'C'. About 1785. 10¾ inches long.

109. Sauceboat with moulded and blue-painted decoration, marked with a capital 'S'. About 1780. 4 inches long.

110. Cream jug printed in blue with a Chinese pattern and marked with a capital 'S'. About 1785. 7 inches long.

PLYMOUTH AND BRISTOL

111. William Cookworthy, 1705–1780, painted by John Opie, R.A.

The researches of a Plymouth chemist, William Cookworthy (Fig. 111), resulted in the making of the only true hard-paste porcelain in England; made in the same manner as that imported from the Far East from a mixture of china-stone and china-clay. It needed a very high temperature for successful firing and this necessitated long experiment, but by 1768 a factory had been opened. This lasted only two years and in 1770 the enterprise was transferred to Bristol.

At Plymouth, the ware was often misshapen, stained from smoke in the kiln and flawed by cracks, but in spite of innumerable difficulties much of the output was excellent. A proportion was painted in blue, often blackish in tone, with Oriental scenes which were popular also on coloured pieces. Figures were made and some of the models were both original and attractive (Fig. 116).

After the move to Bristol, many pieces were based on French patterns and decoration was often fashionably showy with much gilding. Figures, tablewares of all kinds and large vases were produced. In 1781 the company was sold to a group of Staffordshire potters (Fig. 121), and the production of porcelain ceased in the West Country.

112. Sauceboat painted in colours, and marked in red with the sign for Tin. About 1770. 6¼ inches long.

The mark used at Plymouth was the alchemist's sign for Tin, like a figure 4 with a curled front 4
upright. It was also used for a time at Bristol, where they preferred later a cross in blue or gold or
a capital 'B'. As the sign for Tin was employed at both places it is often difficult to decide whether
a particular piece was made before or after the move. Much of the ware from both factories, as from
many others, was unmarked, but in the case of Plymouth and Bristol it can be recognised after a
little experience by its distinctive hard paste.

113. Cup and saucer painted in blue with an Oriental pattern, and marked in blue with the
sign for Tin. About 1770. Saucer, 6¼ inches diameter.

114. Teapot painted in colours
and inscribed under the base:
'Mr. Wm. Cookworthy's
Factory Plymouth 1770'.
5¼ inches high.

115. A mortar, painted in blue
and marked with the sign for Tin.
About 1770. 4 inches high.

116. Group of a boy with a dolphin on a base encrusted with sea-shells and coral. About 1770.
10 inches high.

117. Vase with moulded and painted decoration. About 1770. 12¼ inches high.

118. Figure of a milkmaid and a goat-herd. About 1775. 10½ and 11 inches high.

119. Tureen and cover painted in colours. About 1775. 5¼ inches high.

120. Small bowl painted with an Oriental pattern in colours. About 1800. 4½ inches diameter.   121. Milk jug painted in colours. About 1800. 4 inches high. The men who purchased the Bristol factory closed it and made a quantity of simply-decorated wares from the same formula at the New Hall factory in Staffordshire. In due course they adopted a soft-paste porcelain from which the typical pieces shown above were made.

EARLY NINETEENTH CENTURY

One of the most beautiful porcelains ever made anywhere came from Wales between 1813 and 1822 at Nantgarw and Swansea. The material was white and translucent, and much of it was sold undecorated to be painted in London in the most delicate manner (Figs 122 and 123).

The Derby and Worcester factories made wares of high quality in the fashionable Classical style (Figs 124 to 127), and the Coalport factory, which absorbed those of Caughley and Nantgarw, made well-finished pieces for a large public (Fig. 126). At the Rockingham works, at Swinton in Yorkshire, and in Staffordshire, were factories that catered for those who liked realistic miniature models of dogs (Fig. 131) and homes (Fig. 132); the latter ranging from turreted castles to rose-festooned cottages in which perfume-pastilles might be burned. At Rockingham were made also numerous dessert-services and vases decorated profusely in the taste of the time.

Josiah Spode and his sons had a flourishing factory in Staffordshire where high quality wares were made (Fig. 129), and after being bought by a partner, William Taylor Copeland, in 1833, continues to manufacture to-day under the latter name. Worcester and Mintons (Fig. 130), the latter founded at the very end of the eighteenth century, are also still in production.

122. Swansea spill-vase decorated in gold and dark brown, marked under the base with the name of a firm of dealers PELLATT & GREEN LONDON in red. About 1815. 5¼ inches high.

123. Plate painted with roses, decorated with gilding and bearing the impressed mark NANTGARW C W (the latter for China Works). About 1815. 9¼ inches diameter.

124. Worcester beaker painted in colours within blue and gold borders, and marked with an incised capital 'B' for Flight and Barr. About 1805. 4 inches high.

125. Derby plate with a group of birds painted in colour within a gilt border, marked with crossed batons, dots and a crown in red. About 1810. 8¾ inches diameter.

126. Two-handled mug, or loving-cup, with painted views of Oxford and heavily gilded. Under the base are the names of the views: 'Oxford from the Meadows' and 'Oxford from Iffley'. Probably Coalport, about 1830. 10½ inches long.

127. Worcester cup, cover and stand with feathers painted in colours on a salmon-pink and gilt ground. Probably Chamberlain's factory, about 1810. Stand, 5⅝ inches diameter.

128. Worcester cup and saucer, each in the shape of a tulip and the former with a gilded butterfly handle. Impressed mark FBB, for Flight, Barr and Barr. About 1820. Saucer, 4¼ inches diameter.

129. Spode vase with painted flowers in colours on a dark blue and gold ground. Marked in red SPODE 1166; the latter is the number of the pattern. About 1820. 4¾ inches high. 130. Mintons vase painted in colours with purple-striped double anemones, marked with double 'L' above 'M' in blue. About 1815. 4¾ inches high.

131. Rockingham poodle on a royal-blue cushion. About 1825. 4¾ inches long. 132. Pastille-burner in the form of a cottage. Probably Staffordshire, about 1830. 3¼ inches high.